Jacques Maritain and the Moral Foundation of Democracy

Jacques Maritain and the Moral Foundation of Democracy

JOHN DIJOSEPH

ROWMAN & LITTLEFIELD PUBLISHERS, INC.
Lanham • Boulder • New York • London

ROWMAN & LITTLEFIELD PUBLISHERS, INC.

Published in the United States of America
by Rowman & Littlefield Publishers, Inc.
4720 Boston Way, Lanham, Maryland 20706

3 Henrietta Street
London WC2E 8LU, England

British Cataloging in Publication Information Available

Library of Congress Cataloging-in-Publication Data

DiJoseph, John.
Jacques Maritain and the moral foundation of democracy / John DiJoseph.
p. cm.
Includes bibliographical references and index.
1. Maritain, Jacques, 1882–1973—Political and social views. 2. Democracy—Religious
aspects—Catholic Church—History of doctrines—20th century. 3. Catholic Church—
Doctrines—History—20th century. I. Title.
BX1793.D48 1996 321.8'092—dc20 96–13135 CIP

ISBN 0–8476–8246–3 (cloth : alk. paper)
ISBN 0–8476–8247–1 (pbk. : alk. paper)

Printed in the United States of America

CONTENTS

FOREWORD

The significance of Jacques Maritain is that he introduced one of the central ideas of contemporary political reflection. This is the conviction that political order must be rooted in a spiritual whole beyond itself. Today we talk about the role of religion in public life; previously the issue had been ventilated through the historic controversies concerning church and state. By whatever framework it is addressed the core problematic is the inability of the state to stand on its own feet. Maritain's penetrating grasp of the question has been sharpened by his encounter with states that had sought to constitute the whole meaning of human existence, the totalitarian phenomenon. The appearance of states stridently proclaiming the ultimacy of their new order brought home the radical distortion of humanity they entailed. Maritain was one of the earliest to recognize the totalitarian abyss. It was an extremity that brought the question of the limitation of politics and its transcendent horizon into focus.

It is also an issue at the core of any political order that seeks to maintain limited constitutional self-government. Liberal constitutionalism is premised on the separation between government and a sphere of value beyond it. The difficulty is that the maintenance of that recognition, a form of political self-limitation, is only possible if it is based on something more than political choice or determination. Even in the absence of an institutional check beyond the political realm, there must still be a moral or spiritual reality to define the boundaries of legitimacy. Otherwise there will not only be no incentive for self-restraint, but the state will be unable to identify the fixed points it cannot transcend. Constitutions and bills of rights are indeed "parment barriers" in the absence of an abiding sense of the reality that is their source.

Maritain possessed a solid apprehension of this problematic. He was unlikely to make the error of the legal positivists or of our latter day variants, the deconstructionists, who struggle to assert that an order of law can nevertheless continue without viable means of support. He had seen too deeply into the heart of darkness of political organizations unrestrained by any reality beyond themselves. To the historical liberal skepticism about the good intentions of government he could add the twentieth-century experience of the abyss of evil unleashed by the totalitarian states. It was an encounter that left the indelible conviction, as it did on so many others, that the state must from now on be limited, not merely by its own laws, but by its acknowledgment of an order of reality beyond itself. In this respect he pursued a parallel project to that explored by many of the distinguished Walgreen lecturers, such as Voegelin, Strauss, Arendt, and others, at the University of Chicago around the mid century.

The uniqueness of Maritain was not only his connection with the Catholic and Thomist context, but the explicitness with which he proposed the necessity of looking for foundations within the Christian tradition. Since Christianity has been the major ordering symbolism within western societies all the way up to the present, this emphasis may account for the greater direct influence that Maritain's work has had in actual politics. To refer only to the most evident example, his proposal for the formation of Christianity-inspired associations has received tangible expression in the spread of Christian Democratic parties. Even within the Anglo-American context, where such religiously denominated parties do not exist, the reason is perhaps to be found in the extent to which all the major political parties absorb different strains of the Christian inspiration. One need only reflect on the influence of Christianity within the American civil rights movement or the more recent resurgence of conservative Christian activists to recognize the commonality of sources. In many ways Maritain has had a more substantive sense of the sources of political order than that attained by his more classically inspired contemporaries

The reason for that greater salience is surely his insistence that liberal democratic politics has emerged from a Christian philosophical tradition and must somehow find the way of maintaining that connection under modern conditions. This means maintaining the Christian inspiration within a civilizational context that has become explicitly secular. Maritain's preferred solution is to conceive modernity as a lay expression of the substance that had been overtly religious within medieval Christendom. The point of convergence within the modern pluralist setting could be found, he maintained, within the concept of the person as the source of inviolable dignity and rights. This is a conviction which derives ultimately from the Christian context but has become largely implicit in ways that do not necessarily depend on that explication. It was the core illustration of his proposal that men and women of different backgrounds could reach a practical convergence on principles from which their theoretical divergence could not readily be resolved. An intermediate moral language, in which the recognition could be unfolded, would have to be in the resuscitation of the natural law construction which could stand independent of its Christian theological framework.

The fact that these are precisely the terms in which the issues continue to be debated today is testament to the durability of Maritain's reflections. John DiJoseph's study performs the signal service of placing Maritain within the appropriate context of a discussion for which he was one of the original instigators. Much water has, of course, passed under the bridge since Maritain first broached the question of the role of Christianity within public life, but the realization that we have still not reached anything like a resolution is reason enough to return to one of the first and most perceptive meditators on the problem. Such a course allows us to look again at the achievements and shortcomings which have characterized the effort to define the relationship of the secular state to a transcendent spiritual order beyond it. Maritain exemplifies the issues with a completeness that is scarcely superseded.

The consensus clearly resolves around his major insight that a liberal constitutional order is best linked to its Christian sources through recognition of the transcendent worth of each individual person. This is the point of practical convergence so emphasized by Maritain as the means of remediating the divergence of theoretical justifications. It is the perspective that enabled him to recognize the American Constitution in a memorable turn of phrase as "an outstanding lay Christian document tinged with the philosophy of the day" (Man and the State, 183).

The fact that Americans have ceased to view their Constitution in this way or that Maritain's personalist interpretation of liberalism has not prevailed has much to do with the failure of the argument he has espoused. It is no longer simply enough to point out the Christian ethos that informs respect for individual dignity and rights or to appeal to the cogency of a natural law morality. A way must be found to render the liberal convictions themselves transparent, since it is precisely their viability that is jeopardized by the absence of philosophical justifications. It is surely one of the central strengths of DiJoseph's study that he subjects Maritain himself to that deeper philosophical examination.

DAVID WALSH
Catholic University of America

PREFACE

This book is about the political philosophy of Jacques Maritian, specifically his theory of democracy. Maritain had important things to say about the nature of democracy. What he said is perhaps even more relevant today than in his time with the triumph of what he called "bourgeois liberal" democracy in the United States and Europe, the fall of communism, and the rise of nascent democracies in parts of the former Soviet Empire.

Maritain's political theory has had a significant impact on Catholic and Christian political and social thought. For example, Pope Paul VI in his Encyclical Letter, *Populorum Progressio*, March 26, 1967, ¶ 42, in a paraphrase of Maritain's integral humanism said, "What must be aimed at is complete humanism. And what is that if not the fully-rounded development of the whole man and all men? . . . There is no true humanism but that which is open to the absolute and is conscious of a vocation which gives human life its true meaning." Maritain was the guiding light for the development of this Christian inspired humanism—he called it "integral humanism"—and he was one of the intellectual progenitors behind the formation of the Christian democratic parties in Europe and Latin America in the post-World War II era. Despite his considerable influence, his contributions to the theory of democracy have generally been overlooked.

SPIRITUAL BASE OF DEMOCRACY

Basic to an understanding of Maritain's theory of democracy is his realization that democracy must have a spiritual foundation. For Maritain democracy was more than a system of government, rule by the many. Democracy was primarily a "human way of life." Maritain was referring to one of Tocqueville's central insights about the American democracy, an insight that Tocqueville and Maritain shared and an insight that both believed was applicable to all democracies—that the culture of the social order that undergirds a democracy has a profound influence on the democracy. Tocqueville and Maritain concluded that democracy is unusually susceptible to a culture that fosters materialism. Or, in other words, Maritain and Tocqueville maintained that a democracy must have a spiritual foundation, as will be discussed below.

Maritain rejected the anarchic democracy of Rousseau and what Maritain called the bourgeois liberal democracy of what is now called the modern welfare state precisely for the reason that these two inferior forms of democracy made the spiritual side of man subservient to the material. They exacerbate the natural tendency of democracy for materialism. Maritain foresaw the disastrous consequences that this exaltation of the material would have not only for democracy, but for Western culture generally and for Christianity, for the later was inextricably bound to the Western culture of consumption, at least in appearances. Maritain believed that the bourgeois liberal democracy actualized in the modern welfare state was a "miscarried democracy," infected with "the homicidal error of bourgeois individualism."[1] Not only that, but the Christianity of bourgeois liberal democracy seemed to have forgotten its own social gospel.

Maritain's contribution to democracy is partly dependent on Tocqueville's observations about democracy's tendency for excessive materialism. Maritain saw that democracy would have to be purged of this tendency with its concomitant feature of unbridled individualism. The two fed on each other as Tocqueville had noted.

Maritain was not opposed to materialism or individualism. But, Maritain believed that democracy must have a special kind of individualism, a redemptive individualism that would restrain self-interest, which would combine with a moderate materialism. The redemptive force that would inspire and temper the individual self-interest must be Christianity, at least in Western civilization. Christianity's social gospel emphasized the two defining characteristics of democracy, equality, and freedom. Christian charity could and should be the basis for a body politic grounded on friendship and concord. Christian morality would act as a restraining force on the unbridled self-interest of the democracy's citizens and leaders and also restrain what Maritain called "Machiavellianism" in a democracy's foreign relations, a "Machiavellianism" which was the culmination of the divorce of religion from politics.

Therefore, woven into the warp and woof of the explication of Maritain's Christian-centered democracy is his important and heretofore neglected contribution to the political theory of democracy—that there is a theoretical basis for democracy grounded on man's spiritual nature; that Christianity's spiritual force vivifies democracy as noted above. Maritain's theory of a democracy that makes material values subservient to spiritual values is a viable alternative to the atomistic, rights-driven, oversecularized theories of democracy that have characterized the political discourse of the Western democracies of the nineteenth and twentieth centuries. Maritain believed that the oversecularized theories of democracy lack a necessary feature that every democracy must have—a soul. In Maritain's words:

> The fatality which worked against the modern democracies was that of a false philosophy of life which for a century altered their authentic vital principle, and which, paralyzing this principle from within, caused them to lose trust in themselves.
>
> If the Western democracies are not to be swept away, and a night of long centuries is not to come down upon civilization, it is on condition that they discover in its primitive purity their vital principle which is justice and love, and whose source is of divine origin. It is on the condition that they reconstruct their political philosophy and thus rediscover the sense of justice and heroism in the discovery of God.[2]

MARITAIN'S WRITINGS

Maritain's writings provide the underpinning for this study's analysis and treatment of his idea of democracy. But an examination of his writings is not without problems. Maritain became interested in politics late in his professional career. Events in France in the 1930s and 1940s, including his involvement with the *Action Française* movement, were the precipitators for his interest in politics. Ostensibly, he wrote seven works on political theory, *Man and the State, Integral Humanism, Scholasticism and Politics, Christianity and Democracy, The Person and the Common Good, The Rights of Man*, and *The Things that Are Not Caesar's*. The seven works will be examined in detail. However, the so-called "political works" do not give a complete picture of his political philosophy. Remnants of his political theory are scattered throughout his philosophical *corpus*.

For example, Maritain's political theory cannot be understood without an understanding of his metaphysics. Maritain's neo-Thomism was a precursor of what today is called existentialist Thomism. This variant of

Thomism focuses on action as the revelation of being. It is being in action and being in reaction to other beings that necessitates the formation of a political order. Maritain's political ontology played a critical role in the development of his theory of democracy so, after an introductory theoretical exposition, his ontology will be examined to set the stage for the later specific discussion of his theory of democracy. One of the keys to his political ontology is his *Existence and the Existant*, a work that on its face is not concerned with political theory. The importance of his ontology to his political theory has heretofore not been recognized. As a result, previous studies of his political theory have been incomplete.

Another problem with trying to extract Maritain's political theory from his political writings is that he did not create a formal system of political theory. His political writings are filled with lacunae. A hermeneutic method was used to fill in the gaps. The method is similar to the legal analysis employed to interpret an ambiguous contract. The lodestar in the contract situation is to determine the intent of the contracting parties. Similarly when faced with lacunae in Maritain's political theory the lodestar was to determine his intent. What did he mean? The following procedure was used. First his text was analyzed to ascertain the plain meaning of the language. If the lacunae remained, or if his intent was not clear, reference was made to what in the contract analogy would be the surrounding circumstances, in Maritain's case, his related writings. Nonpolitical works such as *Reflections on America*, *The Range of Reason*, and *Ransoming the Time* were especially helpful. On a few occasions, recourse to the writings of Raïssa Maritain, particularly her *Notebooks*, was fruitful.

If lacunae still remained, recourse was to thinkers who had identical or similar views. For example, Maritain's concept of the prophetic-shock minority was not fully developed. A thinker who had similar philosophical views as Maritain was his contemporary, Peter Viereck, who had written *The Unadjusted Man*. Viereck's unadjusted man is markedly similar to Maritain's prophetic-shock minority so that Viereck's work was consulted in trying to flesh out Maritain's concept. In addition to Viereck, thinkers who had similar views to Maritain and who were used to flesh out his ideas included such diverse thinkers as John Courtney Murray, Fyodor Dostoevsky, and Aleksandr Solzhenitsyn. Maritain's former student, colleague, and a noted philosopher in his own right, Yves R. Simon, was a particularly fertile source for reconstructing Maritain's political theory in general and Maritain's theory of democracy in particular.

Lastly, when necessary to fully develop nuances in Maritain's thought, a comparison between Maritain's thought on a particular subject with a thinker who had views opposed to Maritain's was used. For example, Martin Heidegger's concept of being, which is inimical to Maritain's ontology, provided insights into Maritain's concept of being, a comparison that revealed a link with Heidegger's being and Nazism, in contrast to Maritain's being where the link is to democracy.

ACKNOWLEDGMENTS

It is impossible to list all of the people that contributed in one way or another to this work. I would be remiss, however, if I did not mention Professors Claes Ryn and David Walsh of the Politics Department of Catholic University. Dr. Ryn was an inspiration throughout my graduate studies. Without Dr. Walsh's guidance, encouragement, and constructive criticism this book would have remained an inchoate idea.

Special mention must be given to Dr. Antonio Cua and Dr. Paul Weiss of the Philosophy Department of Catholic University, Dr. Ralph McInerny, director of the Jacques Maritain Center at the University of Notre Dame, Dr. Martin Cohen of the History Department of George Mason University, and Anthony O. Simon of the American Maritain Association, the director of the Yves R. Simon Institute, for his encouragement and help. The conclusions and interpretations of this book are mine not those mentioned above. I also accept responsibility for any errors.

I owe a special debt of gratitude to my wife, Patricia M. Drost, Esquire. Without her support, patience, and encouragement, I would not have attempted a project of this magnitude. She is truly sine qua non.

NOTES

1. Jacques Maritain, *The Twilight of Civilization*, trans. Lionel Hardy (New York: Sheed and Ward, 1944), 57-58.

2. Ibid., 62.

CHAPTER 1

THEORETICAL BACKGROUND

Jacques Maritain claimed a moral superiority for democracy as a form of government because democracy has a symbiotic relationship with Christianity. In Maritain's words, "[I]t is to affirm that democracy is linked to Christianity and that the democratic impulse has arisen in human history as a temporal manifestation of the Gospel."[1] How democracy and Christianity are connected was succinctly and correctly stated, according to Maritain, by President Franklin D. Roosevelt in his State of the Union Address of January 4, 1939:

> Storms from abroad directly challenge three institutions indispensable to Americans, now as always. The first is religion. (It) *Religion* [emphasis in original] is the source of the other two—democracy and international good faith.
>
> Religion, by teaching man his relationship to God, gives the individual a sense of his own dignity and teaches him to respect himself by respecting his neighbors.
>
> Democracy, the practice of self government, is a covenant among free men to respect the rights and liberties of their fellows. . . .
>
> In a modern civilization, all three—religion, democracy and international good faith—complement *and support* [emphasis in original] each other.[2]

CLARIFICATION OF TERMS

Before investigating Maritain's claim for Christianity and democracy, a clarification of terms is in order, for Maritain used "Christianity" and "democracy" in a special sense. The clarification will set the stage for the more comprehensive discussion that is to follow. "Christianity" as used by Maritain included traditional Christian doctrine and what Maritain called a "concrete historical ideal," that is "an ideal essence which is realizable . . . an essence capable of existing . . . in a given historical climate, and as a result corresponding to a *relative* [Maritain's emphasis] maximum of social and political perfection. . . ."[3] The relative perfection that the new Christendom would bring was the actualization in the political and social order of the social gospel of Jesus Christ. The form of government that is best able to actualize Christ's teaching is democracy.

Maritain also gave a special meaning to the word, "democracy," a meaning different from the accepted meaning of rule by the many. His definition of democracy has more than semantic significance. From his definition flow basic concepts about his theory of democracy that are implicated in his claim for the moral superiority for democracy. For Maritain, "democracy" did not necessarily mean rule by the many. Democracy "is first and foremost a general philosophy of human and political life and a state of mind."[4] Democracy in Maritain's sense is a philosophical concept that transcends politics. Democracy is not only a political way of life—a form of government—, but a human way of life. Democracy is a way of living that emphasizes the freedom to choose.

The freedom to choose is the first step in what Maritain called the freedom of autonomy, that is, the freedom of one who has mastery over his own life.[5] This is the first and fundamental level where Christianity and democracy are intertwined. Christianity does not force anybody to do anything. The Christian can choose to live according to the precepts of his faith or to disregard those precepts. The choice is the individual's. In this way, the individual controls his own destiny. In a democracy, similarly, the citizen has the freedom to choose the leaders of the body politic. Maritain thought that this freedom to choose was an inherent freedom in the political as well as in the moral sphere. The two choices are intertwined, for choice, or the lack of choice, in the political sphere could have critical ramifications for the moral sphere. Democracy gives not only freedom of choice, but in addition, freedom of autonomy because each citizen has some control of the political decisions that affect the citizen's life, in contrast, for example, to a monarchy where political decisions affecting the citizen are at the discretion of the king.

Maritain said that "democracy" is also a "social tendency, . . . simply the ardent desire to procure for the working classes, more than ever oppressed in the modern world, the human conditions required not only by charity, but also and in the first place by justice."[6] This is the second level where Christianity and democracy intersect. Maritain saw democracy as the actualization of the social gospel of Christianity, which emphasizes the love of neighbor. What this "state of mind," this "general philosophy" is will be scrutinized in greater detail in the pages that follow. At this point it suffices to say that in Maritain's conception of democracy, the society and, most importantly, the culture should be organized on the principles of Christian friendship and charity, which according to Maritain will inhibit self-interest and individualism, the *bêta noire* of democracy. Because democracy is a state of mind and a social tendency, it can subsist in any of the classical forms of government so that Maritain rejected the numerical component in Aristotle's classical forms of government as being dispositive of the form of government:

> Thus a monarchic regime can be democratic if it is consistent with this state of mind and with the principles of this philosophy. However, from the moment that historical circumstances lend themselves, the dynamism of democratic thought leads, as though to its most natural form of realization, to the system of government of the same name, which consists, in the words of Abraham Lincoln, in "government of the people, by the people, for the people."[7]

A constitutional monarchy, according to Maritain, can be a democracy if the people choose the monarch and the monarch's successor and if the people have certain rights. The critical factor is that in a democracy, as conceived by Maritain, the people are in charge of the government; it is "their" government, the place of power is in the governed. The monarch of a "democracy" is not an absolute ruler. He is subject to the constitution, the law, and is subservient to the people in that he can be held accountable by them.

MARITAIN'S BREAK WITH THOMISM

The placing of ultimate political authority in the people by Maritain represents a heretofore unrecognized break that Maritain had with classical Christian and Thomistic political theory. Although impregnated with the seeds of a nascent democratic political philosophy in the writings of William of Ockham, Marsilius of Padua, and Francisco Suarez, classical Thomistic political theory nevertheless had an absolute ruler at the apex of the temporal body politic. This absolute ruler was unaccountable to the people. He was accountable to divine law and natural law.

The issue of Maritain's fidelity to Thomas Aquinas is beyond the scope of this study. Maritain wrote that it was a given that he did not have a "slavish attachment" to Thomas or Aristotle. Nor would Maritain mechanically repeat another philosopher.[8] Nevertheless, Maritain admitted a "spiritual and ancestral loyalty" to Thomistic concepts that had been proven sound over a course of time. These time-proven concepts provided Maritain with a starting point that he could develop into new solutions for contemporary problems.[9] See, for example, his reinterpretation of the Thomistic thesis of the increase of grace in Christ the man.[10] The process of reinterpretation was also at work in his political philosophy. As a result, Maritain's theory of democracy, his combination of democracy and Christianity, owes its pedigree more to Alexis de Tocqueville and Henri Bergson, rather than to Thomistic political thought, as explained below.

Maritain not only rejected Thomas's—and other Christian political theorists'—claim that monarchy was the best type of government, but in his espousal of democracy, Maritain repudiated what McCool, Adler and Farrell agreed was, to use McCool's language, "an antidemocratic stream" in Thomistic political thought.[11] According to McCool, "Nineteenth century scholastic philosophers, like Matteo Liberatore, had opposed French and Italian representative democracy on the basis of Thomas's social ethics."[12] Maritain's disavowal of the anti-democratic stream in Thomism was somewhat inconsistent. In some of his writings, Maritain defended Thomas's political views. While Thomas did not use the term "democracy," democratic principles were part of Thomas's mixed regime or *polita*, according to Maritain. Thomas's "democracy" was a "sort of mixed system" because "in the abstract [democracy] would tend to the supremacy of mere numbers." Thomas, therefore, tempered rule by the many with an aristocratic and an oligarchic principle.[13]

Adler and Farrell disagreed. They argued persuasively that Thomas's mixed regime had been misconstrued by Maritain and neo-Thomistic political theorists. It was not really a mixed regime but an "intermediate" regime that always included a "monarchical element." Unlike Aristotle's and Cicero's mixed regime, Thomas's *polita* had "always a quasi-royal sovereign man, absolute in power."[14] The absolute nature of Thomas's mixed regime made it inferior in justice and moral value to democracy. Modern Thomists "have tried to make much more out of the mixed regime than St. Thomas's own writings seem to warrant."[15] Thomas's interpretations of Aristotle on political matters were "mediaeval—minded." Adler and Farrell concluded that Thomas was a captive of his historical milieu; he adapted his political theory to the "peculiar institutions of his day, ... his historical location prevented him from being an Aristotelian in his conclusions."[16]

FACTUAL BACKGROUND OF THE BREAK

If Maritain broke with traditional Christian political thought, what were the sources for his espousal of democracy? What were the reasons for his break? His political ontology was an important factor in the break—an ontology that emphasized liberty and equality, as discussed in chapter 2.

Part of the answer lies in historical circumstances, for just as Thomas was a captive of his historical milieu, so was Maritain. He was born in 1882 into a France saturated with the philosophy of positivism, from which he rebelled. French Catholicism, at the time of Maritain's birth and his youth, was caught up in the "adamant anti republicanism of Popes Pius IX and Pius X" that had "allied the Church with the anti democratic forces of reaction."[17] The fortuitousness of being born into one of France's leading, liberal, Protestant families shielded Maritain from the anti-democratic politics of the French Catholic Church. His maternal grandfather, Jules Favre, was a founder of the Third French Republic.[18] Raïssa Maritain wrote "that in Jacques's family tradition the dominant element was an idealistic love of the people, the republican spirit, and the political struggle for liberty."[19]

Doering has traced Maritain's odyssey from a lukewarm supporter of the royalist, Charles Maurras, to his espousal of democracy. Significant experiences included Maritain's involvement in the French Catholic literary revival with his concomitant relationship with Catholic literary figures such as Leon Bloy, Charles Péguy, and Georges Bernanos and Maritain's participation in the founding of *Esprit* with Emmanuel Mounier. A detailed analysis of the political views of the French literati and their influence on Maritain's idea of democracy is the subject of a book in itself. Because Bernanos and Maritain shared common political beliefs, a snippet about their uniformity will serve as a paradigm for the literati's influence on Maritain.

Maritain and Bernanos agreed about the deleterious effect of bourgeois liberal democracy on politics generally and spiritual values; that the people must be supreme in the political order; and that Western culture must be reinvigorated by a new Christendom.[20] In language that mirrored Maritain, Bernanos decried the lack of social responsibility in "the anarchy" of bourgeois liberal democracy. The word "principle" has lost all meaning for the materialistic bourgeois culture. The only remedy is a return to the true principles of the Christian faith, "which requires of me that I love my neighbor, summons me to understand him, which is the surest and most straightforward way of loving him."[21]

It was his experience with Maurras and the *Action Française* movement that "forced Maritain to do some long overdue soul searching about his philosophical indifference to the political realities of life." Maritain was jolted out of his political complacency. His activism of his youth, when he had flirted with socialism, was rekindled.[22] Eventually

Maritain's practiced what he had preached, his existential Thomism led him to conclude that, "a writer whose essential work is foreign to politics cannot, in the midst of a serious crisis, withdraw into that essential work and close his eyes to the anguish of men in the city."[23] Philosophical knowledge, at some point, must leave the speculative realm and act in the practical world. Moreover, Maritain believed that as a Christian he had a special obligation to make his voice heard.[24]

Events outside of France also contributed to the development of his political thought. From 1905 when agitation against the czar started in Russia until his death in 1972, for 67 of his 90 plus years, Maritain watched the world and France battle the forces of totalitarianism, from communism on the left to fascism on the right. He saw France invaded twice, conquered once, then liberated. He was active in the fight against Hitler. During World War II, while living in the United States, Maritain regularly broadcast to the Free French forces as well as occupied France. He also was active in the movement that assisted the escape of European refugees from the Nazis.[25]

The effect that these and other lived-experiences had on the Maritains was alluded to by Raïssa Maritain:

> everything that is in Jacques work, we have first lived in the form of vital difficulty, in the form of experience—problems of art and morality, of philosophy, of faith, of prayer, of contemplation. All of this has been given to us first of all to *live* [Raïssa Maritain's emphasis], each according to his nature and according to God's grace.
> (We began by knowing through experience the absence of truth. Afterwards we began to suffer for It, etc . . .)
> *This goes on* [Raïssa's emphasis].[26]

Maritain's frequent visits to and eventual long residence in the United States sharpened his appreciation of the practical working of democracy. In America, he observed and lived the democratic experience. He described the profound effect that American democracy had on him:

> In actual fact, it is in America that I have had a real experience of concrete, existential democracy: not as a set of abstract slogans, or as a lofty ideal, but as an actual, human, working, perpetually tested and perpetually readjusted way of life. Here I met democracy as a living reality. Residing in this country, and observing with a lively interest the everyday life of its people, as well as the functioning of its institutions, is a great and illuminating, an unforgettable lesson in political philosophy.[27]

Maritain saw that a Christian-inspired democracy was the only answer to the political rapaciousness of authoritarianism of the left or of the right. A Christian-inspired democracy most fit with his political ontology that exalted the spiritual nature of man—the person. It was during the years between the world wars, which saw the rise of two of the great dictators, Hitler in Germany and Stalinist communism in Russia, that Maritain adapted his interpretation of the Thomistic concept of the person to his concept of democracy vivified by the Christian social gospel so that "the genuine, vital principle of a new Democracy, and at the same time of a new Christian civilization can be rediscovered," as an antidote to the mistakes of the eighteenth and nineteenth centuries that produced the totalitarian regimes of the twentieth century.[28] His concept of the person combined with his concept of being, his existential Thomism, formed part of his political calculus. The other part of the calculus, his espousal of democracy, had two roots in political theory. The first root was neo-Thomist, extending from the Spanish version of Thomism of Francisco Suarez back to William of Ockham and Marsilius of Padua. The second root sprang from a French democratic tradition that had historically linked Christianity and democracy.

Two thinkers who had enormous influence on Maritain's development of his theory of democracy were Alexis deTocqueville and Maritain's professor from his student days, friend, and friendly protagonist, Henri Bergson. Tocqueville's influence on Maritain is discussed later. Bergon's contribution to Maritain's political philosophy has heretofore not been recognized because the two thinkers had well-publicized philosophical differences. Yet Bergson's *The Two Sources of Morality and Religion* had a profound impact on Maritain's theory of democracy.

BERGSON AND MARITAIN

To place Bergson in the political tradition of French democratic thought at first glance appears to be a mistake. He was known as a philosopher of science, not as a political theorist. In his last book, *The Two Sources of Morality and Religion*, Bergson contributed to Maritain's philosophy of democracy by giving dimension to Christianity's relationship with democracy. But, even prior to the publication of *The Two Sources*, Bergson's impact on political theory had been and still is underestimated.[29]

In *The Two Sources*, Bergson claimed that society must have a moral order that binds the members of the community. This moral order, or moral charter in Maritain's words, can either be open or closed. It is closed if the moral order comes from within the society, as a result of the society's positive law, its customs, and its mores. Open if the moral order comes from outside society. Because it comes from outside, the open moral order transcends the society, is more universal. The closed moral order is inclusive. It imposes obligations on those within the community by social conditioning. Bergson used the example of the individual ant's duty to the ant colony to illustrate how social conditioning becomes instinctual. All societies, even a democracy, require some type of coordination and subordination, generally through rules and laws. In an ant hill "the individual is riveted to his task by his structure, and the organization is relatively invariable." Although a human community is variable in form from the ant colony, the more "we delve down to the root of various obligations to reach obligation in general, the more obligation will tend to become necessity," and the closer it comes to instinct.[30]

Just as the ant's duty to its colony becomes ingrained, so the closed society exerts continual social pressure to insure conformity with its dictates so that after a time, in some cases a considerable time, conformity becomes instinctual. The closed morality, because it is a creature of the society, serves the society's self-interest by directing individual action to what the society perceives is socially correct behavior, just as the solitary ant instinctively subverts its own interest to the plenary interest of the ant colony due to the threat of punishment by the ant society.[31]

Bergson explained how social pressure enforces obligation in the closed moral order:

> But an activity which, starting as intelligent, progresses towards an imitation of instinct is exactly what we call in man, a habit. And the most powerful habit, the habit whose strength is made up of the accumulated force of all of the elementary social habits, is necessarily the one which best imitates instinct. Is it then surprising that, in the short moment which separates obligation merely experienced as a living force from obligation fully realized and justified by all sorts of reasons, obligation should indeed take the form of the categorical imperative: "you must because you must?"[32]

Here is a practical example of the closed morality at work. In the Soviet Union, political dissidents were silenced by convicting them of crimes against the state under statutes reflecting Soviet positive law and sentencing them to slave labor. By social conditioning by the Communist regime over a number of years, Soviet society not only accepted slave labor as a just and deserved punishment, but attributed moral guilt to the families of the political prisoners, or *zeks* as they were called, in contrast to the political order of czarist Russia where the social mores did not condemn the families of the political enemies of the state. Solzhenitsyn described this process:

> The woman took Nadya [wife of a *zek*] by the sleeve of her coat. My dear! It was easy to love a man in the nineteenth century! The wives of the Decembrists—do you think they performed some kind of heroic feat? Did personnel sections call them in to fill out security questionnaires? Did they have to hide their marriages as if they were a disease? In order to keep their jobs; so that their last five hundred rubles a month wouldn't be taken away from them; so as not to be boycotted in their own apartments, so that when they went to the courtyard to get water people wouldn't hiss at them, calling them "enemies of the people"? Did their own mothers and sisters bring pressure on them to be reasonable and get a divorce? No, on the contrary! They were followed by a murmur of admiration from the cream of society. They graciously presented to poets the legends of their deeds.[33]

Bergson believed that all social conditioning aims at social cohesion, but at the expense of pluralism and decentralization. Because the closed morality demands pervasive conformity through obedience to its dictates, Bergson and Maritain saw that inevitably some type of authoritarian regime must result from the closed morality. The issue was particularly acute for Bergson for any type of authoritarianism would find repulsive Bergsonian metaphysics with its unfettered creativity. The Bergson of *The Two Sources* and Maritain saw a Christian-inspired democracy as the only way to combat the tendency toward centralization, or massification, as Maritain called it, a tendency which was endemic to democracies, according to Tocqueville.

Bergson claimed that all societies have moralities that are partly closed and partly open. The open morality reflects a society's spiritual development at a particular time. Societies are partly open because over and beyond their positive law and customs, they are "overlaid" with another morality, a universal morality that is concerned with what Bergson called "humanity," that is with ends that transcend the ends of the closed morality of society. There is a gap between the closed morality and the open morality in every society. "For between the nation however big, and humanity there lies the whole distance from the finite to the infinite, from the closed to the open."[34] The gap can only be bridged by religion.

> Who can help seeing that social cohesion is largely due to the necessity
> for a community to protect itself against others, and that it is primarily
> as against all other men that we love the men with whom we live? . . .;
> but even today we still love naturally and directly our parents and our
> fellow-countrymen, whereas love of mankind is indirect and acquired.
> We go straight to the former, to the latter we come only in roundabout
> ways; for it is only through God, in God, that religion bids man love
> mankind; and likewise it is through reason alone, that Reason in whose
> communion we are all partakers, that philosophers make us look at
> humanity in order to show the pre-eminent dignity of the human being,
> the right of all to command respect.[35]

Bergson saw certain great individuals—the Greek philosophers, Jewish prophets, and Christian saints and mystics—as mentors, paradigmatic individuals, who showed the way to the open society by their participation in the creative process of developing the open morality. The greatest of the great individuals was Christ.[36] The others are "the imitators, and original but incomplete continuators, of what the Christ of the Gospels was completely."[37] In the political sphere, Bergson saw a creative, evolutionary process from monarchy to democracy:

> It is easy then, to understand that humanity should have arrived at
> democracy as a later development (for they were false democracies,
> those cities of antiquity, based on slavery, relieved by this fundamental
> iniquity of the biggest and most excruciating problems). Of all political
> systems, it is indeed the farthest removed from nature, the only one to
> transcend, at least in intention, the revolution of the 'closed society.' It
> confers on man inviolable rights. These rights, in order to remain
> inviolate, demand of all men an incorruptible fidelity to duty.[38]

The movement to democracy could not be completed without Christianity, "Humanity had to wait till Christianity for the idea of universal brotherhood, with its implication of equality of rights and the sanctity of the person to become operative." Christianity provided the moral justification for the inviolable rights of man and, through its social gospel of universal brotherhood, imbued men with the "incorruptible fidelity" to duty toward each other.[39] Bergson concluded that democracy was "evangelical in essence and that its motive power is love." Evangelical because of the social gospel; motivated by love because of the Christian teaching to love one's neighbor as one's self combined with the Christian concept of the inherent equality of all men.[40]

Bergson's intuitionism had a latent spiritual quality that was only adumbrated in his writings until the publication of *The Two Sources*. The first indication of this spiritual intuition was in one of his earliest books, *Essay on the Immediate Data of Consciousness*.[41] The spiritual part of intuition signified the supremacy of the spiritual nature of man in Bergson's ethics. Although the spiritual intuition was never fully developed by Bergson, it was roughly analogous in concept to Maritain's person. Bergson said that the spiritual intuition "continues in some degree despite ourselves through all the moments of duration in the obscure depths of our consciousness. . . ." The very feeling of duration comes from the continued process of our free activity in the depths of consciousness. The spiritual intuition only acts "in certain cases." The act that actualizes the spiritual intuition must agree "with our most intimate feelings, thoughts and aspirations, with that particular conception of life which is the equivalent of all our past experience, . . . with our personal idea of happiness and honour." The spiritual intuition works in combination with the imagination and reason to create a will disposed to moral action. In effect, according to Raïssa Maritain, Bergson, in this early work, was equating duration with spirit. Her insight is reasonable and justified when combined with Bergson's later more explicit statements in his later works and in *The Two Sources*.[42]

In another comment that hinted at the nature of the spiritual intuition, Bergson, in analyzing the question of the immortality of the soul, wrote:

> Does the soul survive the body? It is easy to decide it once and for all by reasoning on pure concepts. We shall conclude that it cannot be dissolved. Therefore it is immortal. . . . But suppose we give up constructing the idea of the soul as one constructs the idea of a triangle; let us look at the facts. If, as we believe, experience proves that only a minute part of conscious life is conditioned by the brain, it will follow that suppression of the brain will leave conscious life subsisting. . . . It will only be a question of the degree of added life, I admit; we shall have to have other reasons, drawn this time from religion, to arrive at a higher form of precision, and attribute to this life an endless duration.[43]

The left over portion of the brain, the residual consciousness, in Bergson's language, the endless duration, is the soul or man's spiritual nature.

The argument that Bergson's duration is analogous to Maritain's person is further justified by Bergson's claim that duration acts as a restraining force, inhibiting immoral action, in the same way as Maritain's person is inhibited by Christian principles. The restraining force of Christianity is an important feature of its relationship to democracy, for the restraint of Christianity allows the citizen of the democracy to transcend his self-interest. Bergson said that the first characteristic of intuition is "the power of *negation* [Bergson's emphasis] it possesses; it checked the philosopher's will at a given moment and prevented him from acting rather than proscribing what he should do."[44] When faced with the accepted closed morality or the perceived scientific knowledge, the intuition "whispers in the philosopher's ear the word: *Impossible*! [Bergson's emphasis]"

In an article titled "Bergson's Ethics and Morality" published in *Ransoming the Time*, Maritain critiqued *The Two Sources*. He wrote that the book was "most moving of available testimonies to the life of the spirit."[45] Maritain said that although Bergson's philosophical ground for his morality was wrong, when the "spiritual intentions" of Bergsonian intuition were considered, "one must grant that it brings us very precious enlightenment on the subject of the conditions, the environment, the social orchestration of morality, and also concerning its internal dynamism."[46]

Maritain called *The Two Sources* "a classic from the day it appeared, it smashed the narrow framework of the rationalist, idealist, and sociological ethics; it outlined an ethics which does not shut man in on himself, but reveals and respects in him . . . the well-springs of moral experience and of moral life."[47] Maritain equated the closed morality with pressure "which comes from social formations, and from the law of fear." Pressure subjects the individual to "those rules of life imposed by the group and intended to assure its preservation, and which seeks only to turn to the routine and ferocious automatism of matter."[48] In other words, the closed morality is the dominant morality of the democracies that emphasize the material facets of life—the perverted democracies.

Maritain called the open morality "attraction." It comes "from the call of superior souls, who commune with the élan of the spirit, and who penetrate into that infinitely open world of freedom and love, which transcends psychological and social mechanisms; . . ."[49] Open morality invokes what Maritain called a cosmic attitude, "focused upon being," it sees man as transcending his particular group or society, "and sees in the moral life of man, made specific within this universal life by the existence of free will." In contrast, the closed morality is the progenitor of what Maritain called an idealist attitude which "recognizes no other thought but human thought. . . ."[50] The ethics of Thomas Aquinas and Bergson had the cosmic attitude. Open morality and the cosmic attitude are the morality of the spirit, the morality of the personalist and Christian-inspired democracies.

When applied to political philosophy, the intuition of Bergson and Maritain's concept of the person, arrived at the same place from different starting points.[51] For both, politics is a part of ethics. A body politic must have moral stability. And the permanent source of stability must be anchored outside of the law, customs, and mores of the society. Otherwise the morality becomes the acolyte of the society and subservient to it. Dostoevsky expressed the same idea that Bergson was getting at in *The Two Sources*:

> The point, gentlemen, is this: doesn't there, in fact, exist something that is dearer to almost every man than his own very best interests, or—not to violate logic—some best good (the one that is always omitted from the lists, of which we were speaking just now) which is more important and higher than any other good and for the sake of which man is prepared if necessary to go against all the laws, against, that is, reason, honour, peace and quiet, prosperity—in short against all those fine and advantageous things—only to attain that primary best good which is dearer to him than all else?[52]

Bergson and Maritain saw democracy as the form of government that could best allow man to reach the best good and provide long-term stability if the democracy is linked to an ethical or moral order—preferably Christianity. It is only Christianity's social gospel that can undergird the essentials of democracy—liberty and equality. By the time of the publication of *The Two Sources*, Bergson saw that his metaphysics of creative intuition could only be actualized in a democratic political order. His intuition would be completely stifled in a modern autocracy. Whether Bergson regarded democracy as being restricted to rule by the many, in the classical sense, is not known. Given his emphasis on creativity, it is probable that Bergson would have agreed with Maritain that the democratic principle can take root in all of the classical forms of government.

In *Christianity and Democracy*, published about twelve years after *The Two Sources*, Maritain gave Bergson credit for his part in what has become the quintessential theme in Maritain's theory of democracy. Maritain called Bergson's evaluation of Christianity's symbiotic relationship with democracy "profound," because:

> It is the urge of a love infinitely stronger than the philanthropy commended by philosophers which caused human devotion to surmount the closed borders of the natural social groups—family group and national group—and extended it to the entire human race, because this love is the life in us of the very love which has created being and because it truly makes of each human being our neighbor.[53]

Maritain also referred to *The Two Sources* in *Man and the State*. Bergson's claim that democracy's "deepest root" is in the gospel has ramifications for the relationship between politics and ethics. Democracy's leaders must not try to purge the body politic of its spirituality by reducing the democracy to "technocracy." To do so would deprive democracy of its "very blood."[54] Maritain was referring to the excessive bureaucracy of the bourgeois liberal democracy. The passage is significant in the context of the sources of Maritain's idea of democracy because it showed that Bergson and Maritain were on the same wavelength—for the same reasons. They both rejected bourgeois liberal democracy with its excessive materialism.

In a second passage in *Man and the State*, Maritain used *The Two Sources* as an example of correct thinking on how the social bonding of a community takes place. A common governing body does not create a true community. In terms of a world political society, which Maritain was discussing, the passage will be to a large, closed society, "as large as the whole company of nations," then to a large, open society with a corresponding broadening of the concept of civic friendship. The point that Maritain was making using Bergson's open/closed dichotomy was that in the past political societies have been grounded on the closed morality, in many instances by force sanctioned by a society's laws or customs. In the future, political societies will have to be grounded on the open morality that emphasizes freedom.[55]

Did Maritain get the idea of the unique relationship between democracy and Christianity from Bergson? No. As explicated above, Maritain's theory of democracy is a mosaic of the intellectual contributions of several thinkers. However, in the years from 1932 until 1941 when Maritain wrote his major political works—*Scholasticism and Politics, Integral Humanism, Christianity and Democracy, Man and the State*—he had available *The Two Sources* to draw on. That he did so is evident from his remarks about the book and his references to *The Two Sources* in *Christianity and Democracy* and in *Man and the State*.

Bergson's influence on Maritain's theory of democracy has not been recognized. Partly because Bergson was not known for his political philosophy, partly because of Maritain's criticism of Bergson's metaphysics and partly because Bergson was a prime example of his statement that:

> A philosopher worthy of the name has never said more than a single thing: and even then it is something that he has tried to say, rather than actually said. And he has said only one thing because he has seen only one point: and at that it was not so much a vision as a contact: this

contact has furnished an impulse, this impulse a movement, and if this movement, which is as it were a kind of swirling of dust taking a particular form, becomes visible to our eyes only through what it has collected along the way, it is no less true that other bits of dust might as well have been raised and that it would have still been the same whirlwind.[56]

It took the twenty-five years between the publication of *Creative Evolution* in 1907 and *The Two Sources* for Bergson to develop his spiritual intuitionism, although Raïssa Maritain had an early insight about the ultimate direction of his thought. Bergson was using the time between the two books to clarify his thinking. He wrote to Höffding in 1912 that in *Creative Evolution* he had not attempted to deal with "that problem of God" which was "inseparable from moral problems." The short passage in *Creative Evolution* referring to God was only a "stepping stone."[57]

In summary Maritain's and Bergson's theory of democracy are symmetrical in three areas: (1) democracy is the preferred form of political order; (2) democracy must be animated by Christianity; and (3) the spiritual transcends the material in politics. The next chapter will discuss an important aspect of the theoretical background of Maritain's theory of democracy which did develop from his Thomistic roots, his political ontology, and his theory of being.

NOTES

1. Jacques Maritain, *Christianity and Democracy*, trans. Doris C. Anson (San Francisco: Ignatius Press, 1986).

2. Jacques Maritain, *The Twilight of Civilization*, trans. Lionel Landry (New York: Sheed and Ward, 1944), 55.

Franklin D. Roosevelt, "State of the Union Address," 4 January 1939, Speech File, Box no. 43, Folder Title 1191 at the Franklin D. Roosevelt Library, Hyde Park, New York.

Roosevelt's reference to religion's and democracy's relationship to "international good faith" was an echo of another of Maritain's ideas about the relationship between Christianity and democracy—that Christianity enables democracy to fight "Machiavellianism." See below.

3. Jacques Maritain, *Integral Humanism*, trans. Joseph W. Evans (New York: Charles Scribner's Sons, 1968. Originally published in French in 1936), 128.

4. *Christianity and Democracy*, 25.

5. Jacques Maritain, *Scholasticism and Politics*, translation edited by

Mortimer J. Adler (New York: The Macmillan Co., 1941), 138.

6. Jacques Maritain, *The Things That Are Not Caesar's*, trans. J. F. Scanlan (New York: Charles Scribner's Sons, 1931) 131-132, one of Maritain's earliest works on politics, written in response to the Action Française controversy. For Maritain's role in the controversy see Bernard Doering, *Jacques Maritain and the French Catholic Intellectuals* (Notre Dame, Indiana: University of Notre Dame Press, 1983), 6-59.

7. *Christianity and Democracy*, 25.

8. Jacques Maritain, *Antimoderne* (Paris: n.p. 1920) 21 and 263 as quoted in Nora W. Michner, *Maritain and the Nature of Man in a Christian Democracy*, (Hull, Ontario, Canada: 1955), 47.

9. Ibid.

10. Jacques Maritain, *On the Grace and Humanity of Jesus*, trans. Joseph W. Evans (New York: Herder and Herder, 1969).

11. Gerald A. McCool, S.J., in "Maritain's Defense of Democracy," *Thought*, vol. 54, No. 213 (June, 1979): 132.

Mortimer J. Adler and Walter Farrell, O.P., "The Theory of Democracy," *The Thomist* 4: 178 (1941). For three years, from 1941-1944, Adler and Farrell, noted Thomist scholars, wrote a series of ten articles for *The Thomist* in which they set out to prove the moral superiority of democracy. Unfortunately, the critical part of the series where they were to proffer their rationale for democracy's moral superiority was never completed as Farrell was called to service as a chaplain in the United States Navy during World War II. Their articles are an important source for understanding Maritain's political thought for Maritain is frequently cited to support their position, or to criticize the parts of his political theory with which they disagree.

12. McCool, 134. See also Gerald A. McCool, S.J., *Catholic Theology in the Nineteenth Century: The Quest for a Unitary Method* (New York: Seabury Press, 1977) 158-162.

13. *The Things That Are Not Caesar's*, 131.

14. *Thomist*, 6: 66.

15. Ibid., 71.

16. Ibid., 65.

17. *Jacques Maritain and the French Catholic Intellectuals*, 1.

18. Ibid., 2.

19. Raïssa Maritain, *We Have Been Friends Together*, trans. Julie Kernan (New York: Longmans, Green and Co., 1942), 48.

20. See particularly, George Bernanos, *Plea for Liberty*, trans. Henry Lorin Binsee (New York: Pantheon Books, Inc., 1944). An excellent concise summary of Bernanos's politics is Frank O'Malley, "The Evan-

gelism of George Bernanos," *The Review of Politics*, 6, no. 4 (October, 1944): 403.

21. *Plea for Liberty* as quoted in "The Evangelism of George Bernanos," 410.

22. *We Have Been Friends Together*, 41. The Maritains first meeting was at the Sorbonne when Jacques asked Raïssa to join a committee protesting "the ill treatment to which Russian Socialist students had been subject in their own country."

23. Jacques Maritain, *Lettre sur l'indépendance* (Paris: Desclée de Brouwer, 1953) 5 as translated in *Jacques Maritain and the French Catholic Intellectuals*, 60-61.

24. Ibid.

25. Ibid., 168.

26. Raïssa Maritain, *Raïssa's Journal*, presented by Jacques Maritain (Albany, New York: Magi Books, 1973) April 12, 1934, 235-236.

27. Jacques Maritain, *Reflections on America* (New York: Charles Scribner's Sons, 1958), 161.

28. *Scholasticism and Politics*, "Foreword" vii-viii. The American edition of the book appeared in 1941. Maritain's ideas had crystallized by 1938 when the nine lectures that comprise the book were delivered.

29. Henri Bergson, *The Two Sources of Morality and Religion*, trans. R. Ashley Audra and Cloudesley Brereton, with the assistance of W. Horsfall Carter (Notre Dame, Indiana: University of Notre Dame Press, 1979).

For Bergson's influence on French political thought see Richard Vernon, *Citizenship and Order: Studies in French Political Thought* (Toronto: University of Toronto Press, 1986) 194-229. Judith Shklar, in her "Bergson and the Politics of Intuition," *The Review of Politics* 20, no. 4, October, 1958: 634-56, claimed that political theory "must always refer back to some metaphysical presuppositions of *Weltanschauung* that is not itself political." Bergson's metaphysical presuppositions "had its most serious repercussions in the realm of social theory." Shklar claimed that Bergson was the precursor for attacks on social engineering and totalitarianism by "conservative" political theorists like F. A. Hayek, K. R. Popper, and Eric Voegelin. According to Shklar, Bergson directly influenced Georges Sorel and Charles Péguy, and the political and social views of William James. Ibid., 634-635.

As pointed out above, Maritain was greatly influenced by Péguy, who regarded Maritain as a younger brother and protégé. The extent of Péguy's influence is illustrated by Doering's statement that "Three people whom Maritain met within a period of a few years at the beginning of his career profoundly influenced his position on the Jewish Question. In order of importance they were probably Raïssa, his wife; then Léon Bloy, his godfather; and Charles Péguy." *Jacques Maritain and the French Catholic Intellectuals*, 127. See also John U. Nef, "Péguy and the Spirit of France," *The Review of Politics* 5, no. 3 (July, 1943): 377.

Nef listed Péguy as one of "a very small number of thinkers scattered about the Western countries who recognized . . . that Western civilization was entering a period of storm and trouble." Included in the list were T. S. Eliot, Maritain, T. E. Hulme, Tawney, and Sorel. Neff listed four "principal subjects" that the thinkers were concerned with: (1) socialism and the class struggle; (2) the mechanization of labor; (3) religion; and (4) war and nationalism. Ibid., 379.

30. *The Two Sources of Morality and Religion*, 27-28.

31. Ibid., 1-29.

32. Ibid., 26.

33. Aleksandr Solzhenitsyn, *The First Circle*, trans. Thomas P. Whitney (New York: Harper & Row, 1968), 215.

34. *Two Sources of Morality and Religion*, 32.

35. Ibid., 32-33.

36. Raïssa Maritain reported that Bergson had been a secret convert to Catholicism. She did not know the date of the alleged conversion. Bergson's wife released his will to the public after his death. In the will, Bergson said that "my reflections have led me closer and closer to Catholicism, in which I see the complete fulfillment of Judaism." Bergson continued that he would have converted to Catholicism had he "not seen in preparation for years the formidable wave of anti-semitism which is to break upon the world. I wanted to remain among those who tomorrow will be persecuted." He asked that a Catholic priest assist at his funeral. As quoted by Maritain in *Ransoming the Time*, 101.

George Cattaui, a friend of Bergson and a Jewish convert to Catholicism, reported that Bergson said that he believed in the divinity of Jesus Christ and the Catholic sacraments. Bergson died on January 4, 1941, at age 81, from pneumonia after standing in line for hours in Paris waiting to be registered as a Jew as per the dictates of the Nazi-backed Vichy regime. Leszek Kolakowski, *Bergson*, Past Masters Series, Gen. ed., Keith Thomas (Oxford: Oxford University Press, 1986) viii-ix, 86.

37. *The Two Sources of Morality and Religion*, 240.

38. Ibid., 281.

39. Ibid., 77-78.

40. Ibid., 282.

41. Henri Bergson, *Essay on the Immediate Data of Consciousness*

(London: Allen and Unwin, 1910).

42.   Bergson's comments are from *Essay on the Immediate Data of Consciousness* as quoted by Raïssa Maritain in *We Have Been Friends Together*, 93. The contention that Bergson is hinting at the person is based partly on Raïssa's statement that "In other words, this free activity comes first, it is the very life of the spiritual personality, and duration, spirit, and life are synonymous." Ibid.

43.   Henri Bergson, *The Creative Mind: An Introduction to Metaphysics*, trans. Mabelle L. Andison (New York: The Philosophical Library, 1946), 46.

44.   Henri Bergson, "Philosophical Intuition," in *The Creative Mind*, 107, 109-110.

45.   *Ransoming the Time*, 84.

46.   Ibid., 111.

47.   Ibid., 86.

48.   Ibid., 87.

49.   Ibid.

50.   Ibid., 91.

51.   It cannot be emphasized enough that this book is primarily concerned with Bergson's role in the development of Maritain's political philosophy. It is beyond question that the two thinkers' metaphysics were incompatible. Nor is there any question that Maritain was extremely vocal in his criticism of Bergson's philosophy of intuition. See, for example, Maritain's "The Metaphysics of Bergson" in *Ransoming the Time*, 52-83 and his *La philosophie bergsonienne* (1913). Maritain also criticized the intellectual progeny of Bergsonianism. See *The Peasant of the Garrone*, 116-126 for Maritain's strident criticism of Teilhard de Chardin.

52.   Fyodor Dostoevsky, *Notes from Underground*, trans. and intro., Jessie Coulson (New York: Penguin Books, 1972), 30-31.

53.   *Christianity and Democracy*, 53-54.

54.   *Man and the State*, 61.

55.   Ibid., 205-206.

56.   *The Creative Mind*, 112.

57.   As quoted by Maritain in *Ransoming the Time*, 84.

CHAPTER 2

BEING AND THE POLITICAL ORDER

What does it mean to be? To exist? Whatever it means Being must interact with the Other, other beings that exist. The political order has a profound effect on being because it determines the type of relationship that beings will have with each other. A child born in classical Sparta, for example, would have a different being, a different mode of existence, than a child born at the same time in Athens. In the modern world of the second half of the twentieth century to be or to exist without coming in contact with other beings is a virtual impossibility. At the root of all political theory lies political ontology, sometimes couched in terms of a "world view," or theory of being, which tries to answer the fundamental question: How do human beings get along with, or exist with, or be with their fellow human beings?[1]

Maritain's political ontology is the foundation of his political philosophy and his theory of democracy for his political ontology deals with the basic element of his theory of democracy, the singular being and its relationship with other beings.

ONTOLOGICAL PRESUPPOSITIONS

Maritain's ontology and his political philosophy start with a presupposition based on an intuition that things exist:

> Thus Knowledge is immersed in existence. Existence—the existence of material realities—is given us at first by sense; sense attains the object as existing; that is to say, in the real and existing influence by which it acts upon our sensorial organs. . . . Sense attains existence in act without itself knowing that it is existence. Sense delivers existence to the intellect; it gives the intellect an intelligible treasure which sense does not know to be intelligible, and by which the intellect, for its part, knows and calls by its name, which is *being* [emphasis in original].[2]

Here is how Maritain explained this intuition of being:

> Thus the primordial intuition of being is the intuition of the solidity
> and inexorability of existence; and, second, of the death and
> nothingness to which *my* [emphasis in original] existence is liable.
> And, third, in the same flash of intuition, which is but my becoming
> aware of the intelligible value of being, I realize that this solid and
> inexorable existence, perceived in anything whatsoever, implies—I do
> not yet know in what form, perhaps in the things themselves, perhaps
> separately from them—some absolute, irrefragable existence, com-
> pletely free from nothingness and death. These three leaps . . . are
> achieved within the same unique intuition. . . .[3]

QUALITIES OF BEING

Being is not unique or static. "Every thing is being," but each being
differs from each other being; being is "polyvalence." Maritain's use of
the word "polyvalence" reflects his early training in the natural sciences.
He was initially a biologist. "Polyvalent" also demonstrates his reliance
on Being as a ground for his political philosophy. Valence "is the capacity
of one person or thing to react with or affect another [person or thing] in
some special way as by an attraction or the facilitation of a function or
activity."[4] It is this reaction from or acting upon an Other that for Maritain
was the ground for a political order. Being is polyvalent because beings,
by their acts, affect other beings in different ways and, in return, are
affected in various ways. The polyvalence of being is necessitated by the
different species of being and the differences between beings of the same
species. Some beings are human. All beings have an intelligible value that
also varies, also are polyvalent. All the human existents equally
participate in this value in that they all have being. The human existents
act and are acted upon. Action is necessary. By their actions, the human
existents know each other and, most importantly, receive knowledge
about themselves.

"Being abounds everywhere; it scatters its gifts in profusion. This is
the action in which all beings here below communicate with one another
and in which thanks to the divine influx that traverses them, they are . . .
either better or worse than themselves.. . ."[5]   The acts of being have
consequences. "[T]hey exchange their secrets, influence one another for
good or ill, and contribute to or betray in one another the fecundity of
being, the while they are carried along despite themselves in the torrent of
divine governance from which nothing can escape."[6]

For Maritain, being also had a subjective component that has important implications for his political philosophy. Being as subject has two characteristics that affect a political order based on the kind of democracy envisioned by Maritain: uniqueness and freedom.

According to Maritain, man's subjectivity "is linked to the privileges of spirituality and of self immanence proper to personality."[7] Subjectivity is spiritual, the center of man's creative activities, "the source of the super-existence of knowledge and the super-existence of love. . . . a center or universe unto itself of productive vitality and spiritual emanation."[8]

Subject is what exercises existence and action. Each existent is a subject that possesses an essence and "pours itself out in action." Each subject is an "inexhaustible well of knowability."[9] We know these subjects only as objects. As we move up the scale of being from the simple inanimate beings to man, the being endowed with the "perfectly immanent activity of the life of the intellect," the threshold of free choice and independence is crossed. At this point Maritain's subject becomes a person, "that is, a whole which subsists and exists in virtue of the very subsistence and existence of its spiritual soul, and acts by setting itself in its own ends."[10] The person is free and is the noblest and highest in all nature. The existent/subject to itself is the most important person in the world and its destiny is "the most important of all destinies."[11] The existent/subject has an absolute right to control its destiny, a right that extends to the political order.

Subjectivity also possesses uniqueness. No two subjects are alike. Each is different. Subjectivity is the root of individuality, distinguishing each being from each other being. Maritain says that when we first observe a man, we first apprehend him in his universality—as man. His existence reveals his subjectivity, his uniqueness to us. We observe the particular man, Peter, with his particular characteristics.[12] Peter has universal being, but, at the same time, it is his uniqueness as Peter that separates his being from all other universal beings. Peter is Peter, he is not John, or James, or David. Peter has a uniqueness that he shares with no other being, but he has being itself that is shared with all beings. The subject is, of course, also the actor who initiates the activity that reveals being to itself and allows being to know other beings. In the political order the subject is the ground of Maritain's concept of the difference between the person and the individual, a difference that will be discussed later, when the difference between the person and the individual will be shown to be an important difference in Maritain's view of the relationship of the state and its citizens.

EXISTENCE AND ESSENCE IN POLITICS

The action/subjectivity of being is just one root of Maritain's theory of democracy. The human existents/subjects have value. They must act in the sense that they have a natural tendency to act, to interact with other existents. They all reflect into their own being and existence a first being who is Being. They receive through the intellect and give through the will, which, Maritain says, is love. Love "does not deal with possibles or pure essences." It deals with things that exist.[13] The human existents help each other to reach perfection. Perfection does "not consist in copying the ideal; it consists in loving, in going through all that is unpredictable, dangerous, dark, demanding and insensate in love. It consists in the plenitude of dialogue and union with person and person . . .,"[14] eventually transfiguring itself into a form of divine love.

Maritain's politics is concerned with existence. "Political and social life takes place in the world of existence and of contingency, not of pure essences."[15] Maritain continued that "An Ideological politics, be it Jacobin or clerical, knows only pure essences (duly simplified), and one can have a firm confidence that its Platonism will always lead it, with an infallible rectitude to nonexistence."[16] A politics concerned with essences, according to Maritain, is a speculative politics, a politics not grounded on the solid experience of existents, but a theoretical politics:

> In history, as I recalled a moment ago, it is not theses that confront one another, as in a book or an academic discussion, where everything is concluded to the inmost and meritorious satisfaction of the one who is right and who has shown that he is right; it is rather, concrete forces charged with humanity, heavy with fatalities and with contingencies, and which are born of the event and move toward the event, and the existential significance of which the politician has to take into account.[17]

A politics concerned with essences relies on theoretical abstract concepts that have not been tested in the practical political order. A politics of essence posits an ideal, i.e., a political order of the proletariat. In such an order, the essence "proletariat" defines the political system. Everything is constructed around this essence, an essence that is a theoretical construct of what the proletariat is or, more importantly, for the political theoretician, what the proletariat should be, rather than what the elements of the political system actually are, a mixture of existents, each unique. The politics of essences has a preconceived perfect essence and is constructed to produce clones of the preconceived essence.

Maritain's criticism of Blaise Pascal's theoretical approach to politics is a good example of the abstract type of reasoning Maritain opposed because it was concerned with essence rather than existence. Pascal's reasoning had empirical bases. But Pascal abstracted from his empirical bases to get essences. Maritain remarked that Pascal "stumble[d] over all the contingencies of experience, without desiring to go beyond them." Pascal's thinking was flawed because of what he perceived to be, according to Maritain, the "universal depravity" of mankind. Pascal was concerned with "false justice, the justice of the geometricians of non-being. . .; it [false justice] veneers the real with the exactions of an asserted *ideal*, which not springing from things—whose essential ordering it would express—and thus not issuing from divine ideas, is an *idol* [Maritain's emphases], dead and death-dealing."[18]

Pascal is concerned with abstract justice, "geometrical justice," instead of real justice that necessarily involves being; justice as it exists, "of common justice, of justice of root and of sap," justice as it is found in the real world. As a result Pascal compounds his error by lapsing into a type of nihilism since "he deems it madness to become indignant" over the violence and plunder that results from the false conception of justice. Pascal's type of reason is a reason that "face to face with being is solitary; it is not, like nature, bound to a fixed limit; there lies hidden in its structure no submerged regulator capable of re-establishing everything, *in spite of reason* [Maritain's emphasis], order within reason. A boundless liberty is the reason's terrifying privilege."[19]

When Maritain says that Pascal's reason is "solitary" and not nature bound, Maritain means that a politics that is grounded in essences has no bounds to its theoretical constructs. Pascal's type of political reasoning can mentally construct innumerable political theories that have no experiential base. This type of theoretical politics was the intellectual ground for the French Revolution when essences, rather than existence, what actually was, ruled the day. For example, the *sans-culottes* "often estimated a person's worth by external appearance, deducing character from costume and political convictions from character; everything that jarred their sense of equality was suspect of being 'aristocratic.'"[20] The *sans-culottes* did not bother with existence, with the being of their political opponents, with their humanness.

Maritain's words in a different context are equally applicable to the *sans-culottes*, the *philosophes*, like Diderot and Voltaire who were the intellectual progenitors of the French Revolution, as well as the thinkers like Pascal, whose political theories are not grounded in existent being. All of these groups do not respect human dignity in "a real fashion," but in "an abstract, intemporal and unexisting individual" manner that ignores "all historical conditions and differences . . . sacrificing the human substance to anarchic or state-despotic myths. . . ."[21]

MARITAIN AND HEIDEGGER

A clearer picture of how Maritain's concept of being grounds his political theory can be drawn by comparing Maritain's being with the being of another thinker, whose concept of being differed from Maritain's. The thinker is Martin Heidegger. His political ontology led to a political order entirely different from Maritain's type of democracy. The difference starts with the two thinkers' concept of being, which is not to say that there were not also other profound philosophical differences between them.

Heidegger's being had subjectivity and action similar to Maritain's being, but the subjectivity of Heidegger's being was a perverse kind of subjectivity. Indeed, care was the primary attribute of Heidegger's Being, care of the Other. But, it is a dependent care, with overtones of "domination/subordination."[22] Here is one of Heidegger's crucial texts:

> with regard to its positive modes, solicitude has two extreme possibil-ties. It can, as it were, take away "care" from the other and put itself in his position in concern: it can leap in for him. . . . In contrast to this, there is also the possibility of a kind of solicitude which does not so much leap in for the other as leap ahead of him in his existential potentiality—for—being, not in order to take away his "care" but to give it back to him authentically as such for the first time.[23]

Before proceeding with a comparison of Heidegger's concept of caring with Maritain's a cursory look at Being's social relations, as analyzed by Richard Wolin, will put Heidegger's caring in its proper perspective. Wolin, like Dostal and others, is persuasive that Heidegger's Being cannot support friendship and genuine caring as a ground for an ethical and humane political order. Instead, Heidegger's Being can, and according to Wolin and others must, lead to an authoritarian political order similar to Nazism.[24] On the other hand, Maritain's being leads naturally to democracy as will be demonstrated below.

Wolin starts his analysis by focusing on Heidegger's category of "resolve" or "decisiveness" that allows Being, or to use Heidegger's term "*Dasein*," to act resolutely vis-à-vis "They," the others, who are unauthentic because of their indecisiveness. Heidegger said, "For the most part *I myself* [Heidegger's emphasis] am not the 'who' of *Dasein*; the They-self is its 'who.' Authentic Being-one-self takes the definite form of an existentiell modification of the 'They.'"[25] The "existentiell modifica-ation" is necessary because of They's involvement in the mundane, everyday world shield it from the *angst* that infects *Dasein*, so that They cannot become authentic. *Dasein*, however, can free itself of "They" by an act of the will that is absolute in the sense of Nietzsche's will to power.

The relationship between *Dasein* and "They" also involves what Heidegger called the call of conscience of *Dasein*. *Dasein's* response to the call is silence and a drawing back from They. A "smug posture of silent superiority" is how Wolin Characterizes the response, a superiority that is not conducive to solicitude or caring.[26] The result is that *Dasein's* social relations, what Heidegger called "Being-with-others" are inherently unauthentic. *Dasein's* quest for authenticity is aided by its historicity, *Dasein* exits at a certain time and in a certain place. *Dasein* can draw authenticity from its historical milieu by participating as being-with-others in its milieu. Heidegger's being-with-others, Wolin says "codified in ontological form a time-honored commonplace" social division of "German mandarin intelligentsia" of leaders and followers, the leaders have authenticity, the followers do not.[27]

Heidegger's political ontology is reflected in his selective admiration of the Greek political tradition. He was critical of Greek democracy, espousing the view of Jacob Burkhardt and others that the democracy was the cause of the downfall of the polis. According to Wolin, Heidegger's judgment about democratic Athens was extended to his analysis of the modern political project. Athens was a prime example of what happens when the mandarin intelligentsia are made subservient to the uninformed, unauthentic many.[28] Wolin continued that even when Heidegger praised the polis, he did so not from admiration for "its intrinsic political character, that is, the democratic conduct of political life," but only because the polis was the historical place where the "thinking of being" began. Heidegger accepted Nietzsche's characterization of modern democracy as a "degenerate form of the state." Wolin believed that Heidegger's view of Greek society was "parochial" and contributed to his "irrational political judgments," his embrace of Nazism.[29]

A summary description of *Dasein* is Wolin's "joylessness," a joylessness that, according to Guenther Stern, manifests itself in a *Dasein* that:

> suffers from the Christian bad conscience, even from the additional bad conscience of having thrown overboard the Christian concept of sin after all. This doubly evil conscience makes Heidegger's *Dasein* so vile

> that it begrudges itself all joy. . . . No man could bestow a worse treatment on his fellow-man than Heidegger's *Daesin* bestows on itself. Whether the treatment is sadistic or masochistic this question is hard to decide since the social partners are Siamese twins. When "*Dasein*" sleeps, it wakes itself up, if it wants to read the paper it tears this 'tool of mediocrity and average life' from its own hands. It excludes itself from leisure, friendship, friendliness, in short from culture. Its *exercitia* fill the twenty-four hours of the day, its drudgery to march toward death lasts the whole life.[30]

Maritain saw *Dasein's* joylessness from a different viewpoint. He commented that Heidegger's Being is filled with anguish, which Maritain described as "at once keen and lacerating of all that is precious and imperilled in our existence, in human existence." Anguish can be a precipitate of the intuition of being described above, for through anguish "our existence loses its commonplace and acquires a unique value, its unique value. It confronts us as something saved from nothingness, snatched from nonentity." The experience of nothingness can be an introduction to the intuition of being, "provided it is taken as no more than an introduction."[31]

Heidegger went beyond anguish as an introduction to being. Dostal points out that in his lecture *What Is Metaphysics?* in 1929, Heidegger rejected the classical concept of friendship posited by Plato and Aristotle (and Maritain) as an important factor in the political order. The lecture emphasized anguish as the revealer of nothingness. Friendship is conflated with a mood that obscures nothingness.[32]

The key to Maritain's criticism of Heidegger's ontology is Maritain's use of Dostoevsky's term "lacerating," a term Dostoevsky used frequently.[33] Maritain, as an admirer of Dostoevsky,[34] undoubtedly was aware of the particular type of anguish laceration entails, an anguish that affects not only the anguished being, but other beings who have contact with the anguished. Dostoevsky called "laceration" those situations where someone hurts oneself in order to hurt others or hurts others in order to hurt oneself. A joyless, anguished being would have the disposition to lacerate.[35] The hallmarks of such a being are indecisiveness, passivity, and fear of making decisions.

When laceration is added to anguish, the domination-subordination is actualized by the desire to hurt. Laceration is the concrete manifestation of anguish through action against the Other. The anguished fear freedom because to be free, to act freely, requires decisions. The fear of choosing feeds on anguish diminishing the subjectivity of Heidegger's Being so that it is particularly susceptible to the "leap ahead" or "leap in" caring of an authoritative figure willing to make choices.

Heidegger's "leap ahead" kind of caring should be read as the professional kind of caring, a caring, for example, involved in situations where a professional—social worker, psychotherapist, or bureaucrat—"cares" for a client. The goal of "leap ahead" caring is to help the other realize his authenticity by removing a supposed deficiency, unauthenticity, from the other. Unauthenticity is the failure to accept responsibility for one's life. Hence the psychotherapist assists the patient in finding a more authentic existence by helping the patient take charge of the mental or emotional parts of life, just as the social worker adds authenticity to the Other by dealing with the sociability of the other. Being who leaps ahead and the Other are seldom in a position of equality, given the nature of their relationship. The being who leaps ahead generally has the superior position because he has something that the Other lacks, the knowledge or technique that adds authenticity to the Other.

George Konrad's *The Case Worker* is the classic example of the social worker whose "leaps ahead" caring involves a domination-subordination relationship:

> Every day without fail they are here. . . . Their faces change, the grievances are always pretty much the same. . . . How natural they should come and demand attention. As long as this building stands, clients will come here to take up some official's morning hours and entertain him with their problems. Since a client has worries he is defenseless. . . . The official, on the other hand, has nothing to worry about. Impassive, draped in condescending superiority, he has the client—that frail, flustered being who wants something or is afraid of something—admitted.[36]

The other type of caring mentioned by Heidegger, the "leap in" caring "is largely a matter of taking care of the 'worldly concerns' of another, that is providing someone with the things . . . that he or she needs. . . . This relation is inevitably one of dependence."[37] "Leap in" caring can also be interpreted as a kind of sentimental caring or pity, associated with Rousseau who claimed that from pity "flow all the social virtues. . . . Indeed what are generosity, Clemency, Humanity, if not Pity applied to the weak, the guilty, the species in general."[38]

Dostoevsky foresaw that anxious and fearful beings need a "leap ahead" or a "leap in" authoritarian figure who can make decisions, assuage anxiety, and show pity. In "The Grand Inquisitor" chapter of *The*

Brothers Karamazov, the Cardinal, by providing miracles, mystery, and bread, is an avatar of "leap in" and "leap ahead" caring that can be fulfilled by the state, especially the Fascist state:

> Fascism reasserts the rights of the state as expressing the real essence of the individual. And if liberty is to be the attribute of living men and not abstract dummies invented by individualistic liberalism, then fascism stands for liberty, and for the only liberty worth having, the liberty of the State and of the individual within the State. The Fascist conception of the State is all embracing; outside of it no human or spiritual values can exist, much less have value. Thus understood, fascism is totalitarian, and the Fascist State—a synthesis and a unit inclusive of all values—interprets, develops, and potentiates the whole life of a people.[39]

The Fascist state "leaps ahead" or "leaps in" by providing the all encompassing environment mentioned by Mussolini. The Fascist state "cares" for its citizens by dominating every aspect of their lives. The citizens' lives are made more authentic by being merged into the collective of the Fascist state, which expresses the "real essences," not the existences, of the citizens. Maritain's existential being as action or as subjectivity has no place in the Fascist state. The spiritual subjectivity of Maritain's being is completely abrogated by the collective. Being as action is restricted by the tenets of fascism that do not allow free activity.

CHRISTIAN CHARITY AND BEING

The "Grand Inquisitor" model of Heidegger is the figure of the shepherd, a leader figure who also satisfies Heidigger's requirement for authenticity. Man is, for example, "shepherd of being;" shepherds "have the possibility of becoming at home;" they live "unseen and outside the wasteland of the devastated earth."[40] Heidegger, according to Dostal, conceived the shepherd as a poet "who mediates between god and man."[41]

Dostal is persuasive that the shepherd figure is part of Heidegger's faith in a monstrous godlike figure, yet another authentic leader figure for Heidegger. The shepherd has complete domination over the flock and provides "leap in" caring by providing for their physical needs. Heidegger's Being lacks the Christian charity and friendship that is a lodestar of Maritain's being. Maritain's active being imbued with friendship and Christian charity has a decided Dostoevskian character.

Zosima and Alyosha are paradigms of the spiritual values that imbue Maritain's being. Throughout *The Brothers Karamazov*, Zosima and Alyosha exhibit a Christian caring that does not involve domination/subordination. It is a caring that does more than provide for worldly things. It is a spiritual caring, a caring, that Maritain would say flows from the spiritual well of being as subjectivity. It is a caring that exhibits humility, not domination. For example, as a sign of Christian love and forgiveness, Zosima terminates a stormy scene where Dmitri Karamazov has threatened to kill his father, by bowing before Dmitri:

> But this unseemly scene was cut short in a most unexpected way. Father Zosima rose suddenly from his seat. Almost distracted with anxiety for the elder and everyone else, Alyosha succeeded, however, in supporting him by the arm. Father Zosima moved towards Dmitri Fyodorovich and reaching him sank to his knees before him. Alyosha thought that he had fallen from weakness, but this was not so. The elder distinctly and deliberately bowed down at Dmitri Fyodorovich's feet till his forehead touched the floor.[42]

Zosima is the affirmation of Dostoevsky's concept of the spiritual nature made real.

Maritain also affirmed the spirituality of being in his being as subjectivity. It is this spiritual core that is common to Dostoevsky and Maritain that Heidegger's being lacks. Maritain's and Dostoevsky's being do not require a Grand Inquisitor, or a monstrous godlike leader figure to rule the temporal order. Their being looks to a spiritual Being external to the temporal order for authenticity, *the* Being, God, manifested in Jesus Christ.

The difference between Maritain's political ontology and that of Heidegger can be encapsulated in Maritain's explanation of caring. The contrast between Maritain's caring and Heidegger's is stark.

> In the third case, love of friendship for another, the subject tends to perfect the other, also, it is true, himself indirectly. He tends to perfect another, but in a fashion totally different from that of natural agents. For in the case of beings endowed with will, of the overflow of a higher kind peculiar to the order of love, it is a condition of the *gift* [Maritain's emphasis] made to another that the giver has inwardly given himself to the recipient, has in some measure disappropriated himself in his [the Other's] favor, so that he has become another self. It is in this that the overflow, distinctive of love, essentially consists.[43]

For Maritain caring is a gift. Part of the gift is that the giver gives of himself to the recipient. The giver has dis-appropriated, taken something from himself, some part of himself, to make the other more perfect, not to enhance the other's authenticity. The giver "tends inwardly toward his friend as towards a second self. And in virtue of his love for his friend he will act. He will and do what is good for his friend."[44]

NATURAL COMMUNITY OF ACTION AND REACTION

In contrast to Heidegger, Maritain's beings have an existential bond between themselves and the other human existents who compose the political order because their relationship is not one of domination and subordination. A natural community of action and reaction is created. The existents through this existential bond unite in a political order, but this bond, this community, is prior to the formation of the political order. The community has been inchoate. The establishment of the political order develops what was an inchoate existential bond into a political bond that forms a political community.

Why is the existential bond necessary? Why must it develop? Maritain explains that the person:

> by virtue of his dignity, as well as his needs, requires to be a member of society. . . . He demands this, first by virtue of the very *perfections* which are inherent in him, and because of the fact of this being open to communications of knowledge and of love . . ., and which require an entrance into relations with other persons. . . . And secondly, it is because of his *needs* that the human person demands this life in society. Taken in the aspect of his indigences, he demands to be integrated to a body of social communications, without which it is impossible for him to attain to his full life and achievement. [Maritain's emphases] [45]

Political order would naturally develop, according to Maritain, even if the community were composed of perfectly intelligent and perfectly informed human beings. The only inchoate community which would not develop into a political community is one whose members are not only perfectly intelligent and perfectly informed, but also perfectly virtuous. As Maritain explained in his review of Simon's book *Nature and Functions of Authority*:

> Now this seems to be certainly true even of perfectly intelligent and
> perfectly well-informed men [that Simon's statement that political
> order would be necessary]. But if they are at the same time *perfectly
> virtuous*, what must we say? Prudence as such is infallible; therefore if
> we suppose two men perfectly intelligent, well-informed and *virtuous*,
> placed in the same community. . . . we should say that in [such] a
> community . . . there will surely be agreement among them in the
> prudential judgments concerning the good of this community,—an
> agreement which is not due to any demonstration, but to their common
> rightness of their appetite for the end [emphases are Maritain's].[46]

For Maritain political order is not based on a social contract that
develops from a prepolitical state of nature; nor does political order
necessarily rise because of man's depraved nature; nor is political order
necessary to protect private property and to provide impartial judges to
litigants in disputes over property. Political order precedes the social
contract; political order flows from the interactions of being. Political
order is natural.

> Thus social life remains the life natural to man, required by his deepest
> spiritual needs. . . . It is social life which leads to the life of the spirit;
> but by that very ordination just as the activity of reason is ordered to
> the simple act of contemplation, so the social life is ordered to the
> solitary life, to the imperfect solitude of the intellectual, to the solitude,
> perfect, at least interior of the saint.[47]

In this passage, Maritain, in addition to emphasizing the naturalness
of the political order, adumbrates another key element of his political
philosophy—the earthly social and political order plays a key role in
man's salvation or condemnation, by providing an environment where
man's spiritual life can flourish or stagnate. A citizen of a regime
dominated by anthropocentric humanism, or a regime hostile to
Christianity, such as existed until recently in the Soviet Union, has a more
difficult road to eternal salvation than a citizen of a regime that respects
and encourages the spiritual development of its citizens. "The human
person cannot achieve his fullness alone, but only through receiving
certain goods essential to him from society." Society is required to
"accomplish human dignity."[48]

In his belief in the naturalness of the political order, Maritain is
Aristotelian. He would agree with Aristotle that man is "by nature a
political animal," and that a man who by nature is without a state is living
in an unnatural or perverted manner, a "bad man," or is a god, "above

humanity."[49] The homeless, stateless man who, according to Aristotle, was denounced by Homer "may be compared to an isolated piece of draughts,"[50] a man without any support, drifting. Such a man is not human.[51] Maritain would add that the isolated man cannot know himself or others because he has no one to react with.

Maritain, by positing a natural necessity for the political order, broke with the political theory of St. Augustine. Since the political order is natural and necessary, it does not exist to act as a restraining force on man's evil desires, or as a defense against foreign invaders as Augustine maintained.[52] Original sin made a coercive political order necessary, according to Augustine. As a result of man's fall, the world is divided into two cities, a city of God whose citizens follow the teaching of Jesus Christ, and a city of man, an earthly city devoted to the material world. The city of man needs a coercive political order; the city of God does not.

The difference between Maritain and Augustine can be crystallized: for Augustine politics was not relevant to man's ultimate end—salvation. The political order was something that had to be endured by the Christian as he journeyed through life. It was functional in that it imposed order upon depraved man. The political order did not, could not, play a positive role in the journey to salvation. At best, the political order would not impede the Christian's journey by persecuting Christianity as some of the Roman Emperors had done.

No temporal state could be a true commonwealth for no state can have true justice, a justice which only comes from serving God. "Because if this is so, what fragment of justice can there be in a man who is not subject to God. . . . And if there is no justice in a man of this kind, then there is certainly no justice, either, in an assembly made up of such men."[53]

Maritain was more sanguine about the state. He certainly would agree with Augustine about the effect of original sin on human nature. He also would agree with Augustine that the coercive power of the state was necessary at times to restrain those who could not restrain themselves. However, instead of an indifference to the state on the part of Christians, Maritain saw Christianity as a vivifying force within the state, a positive force that would provide the ethical ground for governance. Rather than limit the participation of the Christian in the political order to political issues that directly affected religion, such as the defense of religious freedom, Maritain believed that the active participation of the Christian in politics was not a question of choice, but a duty:

> Such an activity [defense of religious freedom] is certainly indispensable, it is necessary; it is not sufficient. It imperatively

requires the Christian; he must not limit himself to it. He must not absent himself from any domain of human action, he is needed everywhere. He must work at once—inasmuch as he is Christian—on the plane of religious action (which is indirectly political), and inasmuch—as he is a member of the spiritual community—on the plane of action which is properly and directly temporal and political.[54]

The duty that Maritain claims of the Christian to participate by action in the political process requires means through which the required action can be made manifest. The means most suited to the ends of Christian action are the nonviolent techniques developed by Mahatma Gandhi, as discussed below.

CHRISTIANITY AND POLITICAL BEING

This positive force of Christianity is itself grounded in Maritain's concept of being as stated above, for being with value, created by God, must play a role, according to its very existence, manifested in its action and subjectivity, in political decisions. Maritain succinctly described this relationship as follows:

> These two images—of myself and of my situation in respect of other subjects—can positively not be superposed. These two perspectives cannot be made to coincide. I oscillate rather miserably between them. If I abandon my self to the perspective of subjectivity, I absorb everything into myself [Rousseau], and, sacrificing everything to my uniqueness, I am riveted to the absolute of selfishness and pride. If I abandon myself to the perspective of objectivity, I am absorbed into everything, and dissolving into the world, I am false to my uniqueness and resign my destiny. It is only from above that the antimony can be resolved. If God exists, then not I, but He, is the center; and this time not in relation to a certain particular perspective. . . . and because unimportant as I am in the world, I am important to Him; not only I, but all the other subjectivities whose lovableness is revealed in Him and for Him, and which are henceforward together with me, a *we*, called to rejoice in His life.[55]

In the political order, one who is immersed in subjectivity is consumed with its own self-interest. Being immersed in subjectivity was the ground for Plato's criticism of democracy. The many immersed in their own self-interest cannot act for the common good. They are so absorbed with themselves that their subjectivity interferes with their capacity to set aside their own self-interests, their subjectivity dominates. Maritain's ontology, as it relates to politics, should be interpreted historically; that is, being immersed in subjectivity has led to an atomistic individualism, or subjectivity allowed itself to be unduly influenced and controlled by the Other's subjectivity. When the Other's subjectivity dominates being, being immersed in subjectivity's inchoate existential bond develops into a pseudocollective that is dominated by an authoritarian figure.

On the other hand, being immersed in objectivity merges with the collective so that the common good is identical with a collective common good, i.e., the good of the Communist Party, or National Socialism. Being immersed in objectivity is subordinated to the collective; being in this situation gives up its subjectivity to a collective subjectivity of the community.

Being immersed in collectivity is, according to Maritain, one of the central flaws in what could be called Marx's political ontology. Marx made man "a particle of the social whole and lives on the collective consciousness of the whole, and his happiness and liberty lie in serving the work of the whole." Man still has the "thirst for communion," the natural inclination for sociability described above, but the "communion is sought in economic activity, in pure productivity. . . ."[56]

Maritain saw Christianity as the mediator between being immersed in subjectivity and being immersed in objectivity. Through the social teaching of the gospel inordinate subjectivity is required to put aside its particularity and uniqueness to work for the common good of all. Conversely, the Christian social gospel also emphasizes uniqueness, particularity within the collective so that the individual cannot be subsumed within the collective.

It is Maritain's concept of a redemptive individualism that undergirds his Christian-inspired democracy. The individual in his democracy is not the self-centered individual of Plato's democracy, nor the atomistic individual of bourgeois liberal democracy. The redemptive individual is mandated by his Christian faith to care for his neighbors so that the redemptive individual's Christianity cools the fire of self-interest.

Because Maritain's ontology emphasizes being that is free and of equal value with other beings, it is only a pulsebeat from a political philosophy of democracy. The acting, unique, and free person of Maritain's ontology could function best in a political order where such a person had control of its own destiny by participating in the political order.[57]

This study agrees with Dennehy's conclusion about the effect of Maritain's ontology on his politics, although Dennehy would claim that it is Maritain's Thomism that is the ground for the relationship between his ontology and politics, including his espousal of democracy. "Thomism [not just Maritain's interpretation of Thomism] achieves a fusion between the necessity and universality of essence on the one hand and the contingency, uniqueness, and freedom of existence on the other." Because subjectivity is grounded in existence, "it is no accident" that [Maritain's] social and political philosophy is "libertarian and progressive, despite its grounding in the Natural Law and the universality of human nature."[58] Maritain's politics grounded in an ontology that emphasizes being's uniqueness, freedom, and spirituality combined with the Christian command to love one's neighbor as one's self is actualized most fully in a democracy, not just any democracy, however, but a Christian-inspired democracy. In contrast, Heidegger's being grounded in domination-subordination, according to Strauss, Adorno, and others, is a "straight line" that connects Heidegger's philosophy and his authoritarian politics.[59]

I agree with Dennehy's conclusion, but disagree with his rationale. Maritain's conception of democracy is a combination of his neo-Thomistic ontology combined with his break with classical Thomistic political thought supplemented partly by his interpretation of Tocqueville and Bergson.

NOTES

1. This chapter is limited to a discussion of Maritain's ontology in so far as it relates to his political philosophy. Being as the foundational element in Maritain's political philosophy is derived from a neo-Thomistic metaphysics that today is referred to as "existentialist Thomism," a neo-Thomism that stresses the primacy of existence over essence and action as the self-revelation of being. See, for example, *Summa contra Gentiles*, Bk. II, ch. 79; W. Norris Clarke, S.J., "Action as the Self Revelation of Being; a Central Theme in the Thought of St. Thomas," Linus Thro, ed., *History of Philosophy in the Making. In Honor of James Collins* (Lanham, Maryland.: University Press of America, 1982), 68; and Gerald A. McCool, S.J., ed., *The Universe as Journey: Conversations with W. Norris Clarke, S.J.* (New York: Fordham University Press, 1988). Clarke is one of the chief proponents of existentialist Thomism.

Although Maritain's espousal of democracy was a break with classical Thomist and Christian political philosophy as noted above, his metaphysics was grounded in classical Thomism.

2. Jacques Maritain, *Existence and the Existent*, English version by Lewis Galantiere and Gerald B. Phelan (Lanham, Maryland: University Press of America, 1975), 11, 28-32.

3. Jacques Maritain, *Approaches to God*, trans. Peter O'Reilly (New York: Harper and Brothers, 1954), 3.

4. Jacques Maritain, *An Introduction to the Basic Problem of Moral Philosophy*, trans. Cornelia N. Borgerhoff (Albany, New York: Magi Books, 1990), 29.

The Random House Dictionary of the English Language, 2nd ed., unabridged (1987), s. v. "valence."

5. *Existence*, 42.

6. Ibid., 43.

7. See Jacques Maritain, "Poetic Experience," *The Review of Politics,* vol. 6, no. 4 (October, 1944): 387, 393.

8. Ibid.

9. *Existence*, 63-66.

10. Ibid., 68.

11. Ibid., 75.

12. Jacques Maritain, *An Introduction to Philosophy*, trans. E. I. Watkin (New York: Sheed and Ward, 1930), 164, 168-69.

13. *Existence*, 49.

14. Ibid., 50.

15. *Integral Humanism*, 219.

16. Ibid., 220.

17. Ibid.

18. Jacques Maritain, "The Political Ideas of Pascal," *Ransoming the Time* (New York: Charles Scribner's Sons, 1941), 34, 37-38.

19. Ibid., 41, 43, 45.

20. Albert Soboul, *The Sans-Culottes*, trans. Remy Inglis Hall (Princeton, New Jersey: Princeton University Press, 1980), 3.

See also Edmund Burke, *Reflections on the Revolution in France* (Buffalo, New York: Prometheus Books), 129, 170. Burke excoriated the revolutionary leaders for their "untried speculations" and "loose theories."

21. *The Twilight of Civilization*, 59.

22. Robert Dostal, "Friendship and Politics. Heidegger's Failing," *Political Theory*, vol. 20, No. 3 (August, 1992): 399, 408.

23. Martin Heiddeger, *Sein und Zeit* (Tubingen: Niemeyer, 1967) 122, in English, *Being and Time*, trans. John Macquarrie and Edward

Robinson (New York: Harper & Row, 1962), 158-59.

24. Dostal points out that such diverse political theorists as "Theodor Adorno and Leo Strauss have long argued a straight line from Heidegger's philosophy to fascism, if not an identity." Dostal sees no "straight line," but believes "there might well be a crooked one." Dostal, 399.

Dostal cites Leo Strauss, "A Giving of Accounts," *The College* 22 (Annapolis and Santa Fe no. 1, 3, and T. Adorno, *Jargon der Eigenlichkeit* (Frankfurt: Suhrkamp, 1964).

25. See Richard Wolin, *The Politics of Being: The Political Thought of Martin Heidegger* (New York: Columbia University Press, 1990), 35; *Being and Time*, 312.

It is beyond caveat that Heidegger willingly and fervently embraced National Socialism. The only question is: Was Heidegger's commitment to National Socialism tied to his philosophy?

Some examples provided by Wolin that illustrate the fervor of Heidegger's commitment are:

1. While Rector at Freiburg, Heidegger aggressively implemented Hitler's policy of eliminating the Nazi's political opposition.

2. In November 1933, Heidegger made three public appeals in support of Hitler.

3. Heidegger made membership in the National Socialist Party a prerequisite for the professorship.

4. In December 1933, Heidegger circulated a memo to all university deans that stated Heidegger's unequivocal goal of his rectorship was "the fundamental transformation of scholarly education on the basis of the forces and demands of the National Socialist State. . . . The individual himself counts for nothing. The fate of our *Volk* in its State counts for everything."

5. On numerous occasions Heidegger exhibited a virulent anti-Semitism. *Politics of Being*, 1-15.

I have parsed Wolin's analysis to the minimum necessary to provide a comparison between Maritain's and Heidegger's ontology so that the differences in their political philosophy can be highlighted.

26. *The Politics of Being*, 42-44.

27. Ibid., 55-56.

28. Ibid., 87-88. Wolin's statement is based on Martin Heiddeger's *Was heisst Denken*? (Tübingen: M. Neimeyer, 1954), 65.

29. Ibid.

30. Guenther Stern, "On the Pseudo-Concreteness of Heidegger's Philosophy," *Philosophy and Phenomenlogical Research* 9 (1948), 337, 362.

31. Jacques Maritain, *A Preface to Metaphysics: Seven Lectures on Being* (New York: Sheed and Ward, 1938), 50.

32. Dostal, 410.

33. See Fyodor Dostoevsky, *The Brothers Karamazov*, trans. Constance Garnett, revised by Ralph Matlaw (New York: W. W. Norton & Company, 1976), particularly Book IV "Lacerations."

34. Here are two examples among several where Maritain and Dostoevsky are in agreement are: *Integral Humanism*, 60; Dostoevsky had "profound intuition," portrayed through Kirilov in *The Possessed*, that atheism "provokes in the end psychic dissolution;" *Integral Humanism*, 105; Dostoevsky's "Legend of the Grand Inquisitor" exposes the "theocratic error" that absolute happiness is possible in the temporal world. For an analysis of Dostoevsky's spiritual vision see George A. Panichas, *The Burden of Vision* (Chicago: Regnery Gateway, Inc., 1985); David Walsh, *After Ideology: Recovering the Spiritual Foundations of Freedom* (San Francisco: Harper-Collins, 1990).

Maritain's and Dostoevsky's political philosophy were isomorphic. They both grounded their politics in Christianity, Maritain in the Catholic Church, Dostoevsky in the Russian Orthodox Church. They both opposed the rationalistic, utopian political philosophies exemplified by thinkers like Comte, Chernyshevsky, Marx, and Lenin. Maritain and Dostoevsky differed in their attitude toward the Catholic Church, however, Dostoevsky was virulently anti-Catholic. See Denis Dirscherl, S.J., *Dostoevsky and the Catholic Church* (Chicago: Loyola University Press, n.p.)

35. Also Robert Belknap, "The Structure of Inherent Relationships: The Buffoon, the *Nadryv* (Laceration)," *The Structure of the Brothers Karamazov* (The Hague: Mouton and Co., 1947) 41-47. *Nadryv* can also be translated as anguish.

36. See George Konrad, *The Case Worker*, trans. Paul Aston, intro. Irving Howe, the Writers from the Other Europe series, Philip Roth, general ed. (New York: Penguin Books, 1987), 14. See also James Burnham, *The Managerial Revolution* (Westport, Connecticut: Greenwood Press, 1972).

Significantly, Maritain opposed the oppressive power of the state's bureaucracy that is characteristic of "leap ahead" caring.

37. Dostal, 406.

38. Jean-Jacques Rousseau, *Discourse on the Origin and the Foundations of Inequality Among Men*, trans. and ed. Victor Gourevitch, Part I, ¶ 37 (New York: Harper & Row, 1986). See also Irving Babbitt, *Rousseau and Romanticism*, intro. Claes Ryn (New Brunswick, New Jersey:

Transaction Publishers, 1991); Irving Babbitt, *Democracy and Leadership*, foreword by Russell Kirk (Indianapolis, Indiana: Liberty Classics, 1979).

39.   Benito Mussolini, *Fascism: Doctrine and Institutions* (Rome: "Ardita" Publishers, 1935) 10.

40.   Martin Heidegger, "Letter on Humanism," *Basic Works*, trans. Frank Capuzzi and J. Glenn Gray, ed. David Krell (New York: Harper & Row, 1977) 232, 235-36; see also Martin Heidegger, "Understanding Metaphysics" *Vortrage und Aufsatze* (Pfullingen; Neske, 1954): Dostal, 414, 423, n. 41.

41.   Dostal, 443, n. 41, 42.

42.   *The Brothers Karamazov*, 65.

43.   *A Preface to Metaphysics*, 72.

44.   Ibid., 115.

45.   *Scholasticism and Politics*, 3rd ed. (1954), 54.

46.   *The Review of Politics*, vol. III, no. 2 (April, 1941): 250-54.

47.   Also Jacques Maritain, *Three Reformers* (New York: Sheed and Ward, 1950), 123.

48.   *Scholasticism and Politics*, 68-69.

49.   Aristotle *Politics,* bk. 1, ch. 2.

50.   Ibid.

51.   Ibid.

52.   Augustine, *City of God*, XIV, 1; Ibid., XXII, 22; Ibid., IV, 15.

53.   Ibid., XIX, 22. See Herbert A. Deane, *The Political and Social Ideas of St. Augustine* (New York: Columbia University Press, 1963).

54.   *Integral Humanism*, 258.

55.   *Existence*, 75-76.

56.   Jacques Maritain, *The Range of Reason* (New York: Charles Scribner's Sons, 1952), 190.

57.   I have parsed Maritain's ontology to what is necessary for an understanding of his political theory because I am interested in his ontology only as it relates to his political theory. For a detailed discussion questioning whether Thomism is "as Maritain interpreted it—really an existentialism?" see, for example, Raymond Dennehy, "Maritain's Theory of Subsistence: The Basis of His Existentialism," *The Thomist* 39 (1979): 542.

58.   Ibid.

59.   See Fred Dallmayr, "Ontology of Freedom: Heidegger and Political philosophy," *Polis and Praxis* (Cambridge: MIT Press, 1984). Dallmayr maintains that Heidegger contributed to "dislodging . . . freedom from human willfulness and subjectivity." Ibid., 129.

Also, Victor Farias, *Heidegger and Nazism*, ed. Foreword, Joseph Margolis and Tom Rockmore. French materials trans. Paul Burrell and Dominic DiBernardi. German materials trans. Gabriel R. Ricci (Philadelphia: Temple University Press, 1989). French edition, *Heidegger et le nazisme* (Paris: Editions Verdier, 1987).

Karl Löwith, in his autobiography *Mein Leben in Deutschland vor und nach 1933* (Stuttgart: Metzler, 1986), 57, claims that in a conversation with Heidegger in 1936, Heidegger admitted his fidelity to Hitler and that his National Socialism was the essence of his philosophy.

CHAPTER 3

THE PERSON

The *excursus* into Maritain's ontology concluded by showing a nexus from his ontology to his political philosophy. Now that nexus will be expanded to include his conception of democracy. The expanded nexus that unites being and democracy is Maritain's idea of the person, the spiritual side of being as subjectivity, as opposed to the individual, the material side of being as subjectivity. When the person is the north star of a democratic political order, the citizens are united by a common moral charter in what Maritain calls a personsalist democracy.[1] When the person is relegated to an inferior position in a democracy the regime is what Maritain called anarchic democracy, as will be more fully explained below. The person is the glue that unites the two cornerstones of Maritain's political philosophy, being and democracy, by fusing the spirituality of being and the spirituality of the Christian religion. A type of democracy emerges that Maritain thought could best protect and develop the spiritual nature of man, which, for him, is the *sine qua non* for the existence of a body politic.

The person and individual are related to being. Maritain referred to them as "metaphysical aspects" of the human being. Each has its own "ontological physiognomy" that will now be analyzed.[2]

THE PERSON AND LOVE

The key that unlocks the "profound significance" of the person is "to consider the relation between personality and love."[3]

> Love does not aim at qualities, one does not love qualities. What I love is the deepest reality, the most substantial, hidden *existing* [Maritain's emphasis] reality in the beloved—a metaphysical centre, deeper than all qualities and essences which I can discover and enumerate in the beloved. That is why such enumerations pour endlessly from the lover's mouth.

> Love aims at this center, without separating it from the qualities—in fact, merging into one with them. This center is in some way inexhaustibly a source of existence, of goodness and of action, capable of giving and of *giving it-self* [Maritain's emphasis]—and capable of receiving not only this or that gift from another, but another self as gift and giver.[4]

The nexus between Maritain's ontology and the person is evident. The person first and foremost exists. The person is not essence or qualities. The person gives and receives, gives itself through love, receives the Other through love. For Maritain love is manifested through friendship and Christian charity. The person exists in a special way, for in order "to be able to *give oneself*, one must first exist, and not only as the sound which passes in the air, or this idea which crosses my mind, but as a thing which . . . itself exercises existence."[5] The person has to exist in an "eminent way, by possessing itself, by holding oneself in hand and by disposing of oneself; that is one must exist through a spiritual existence, capable of enveloping itself by intelligence and freedom. . . ."[6]

A "spiritual existence" is necessary because without it the human being cannot "envelope" itself, cannot surround itself, cannot become a spiritual core through its knowledge of the spiritual and its free choice of the spiritual. One of the ways that the person is an envelope for itself is through a sense of what is good, what is right, and what is wrong. When Maritain speaks of the person "possessing itself," he means that the person has self consciousness. The person is "exercising existence" when acting through its own self-determination. The person, in the well of spirituality that is at its core, can determine for itself, without interference from the Other, how and when it will act.

The person's spiritual existence constitutes its core. By existing spiritually, the person is real, an independent whole, "a universe by itself, . . . facing the transcendent Whole, which is God." Person is the "highest and deepest dimensions of being," its roots go to the deepest depths of spirituality.[7] The person has the freedom of choice to control its own destiny by the exercise of its freedom. "Neither nature nor the State can lay prey to this universe" without the person's permission. Even God, "who is and acts within [the independent universe]" does so with an "exquisite delicacy, which shows the value He sets on it; He respects its freedom; . . . He never forces it."[8]

The spirituality of the person is relative to the absolute. This relationship gives the person value. Only through the absolute can the person find fulfillment because:

the human person not only bears to God the common resemblance born by other creatures; it resembles Him in a proper and peculiar fashion. It is the image of God. For God is spirit, and the person proceeds from Him, having as its principle of life a spiritual soul, a spirit capable of knowing and loving, . . . so to finally love Him and know Him even as He knows and loves Himself.[9]

The person's symbiotic relationship with a transcendent Being has three important consequences for Maritain's political philosophy and his conception of democracy, which will be discussed below: (1) the person has a connection with Christianity for it is the Christian God that created the person and to whom the person is bound; (2) the person has an inherent dignity that is ultimately grounded in the spiritual, which is also a result of the person's connection to the Christian God; and (3) it is the person who possesses certain rights against the state; rights that spring from the person's spirituality.

THE INDIVIDUAL

While being is preeminently spiritual as person, there is a material element in being, called individuality by Maritain, that also must be recognized. Only individuals are capable of exercising the act of existing. The ontological physiognomy of individuality is marked by exclusiveness. Maritain described it as "the narrowness in being."[10] It is being:

opposed to the state of universality which things have in the mind. It [individuality] designates the concrete state of unity and indivision, required by existence, in virtue of which every actually or possible existing nature can posit itself in existence as distinct from other beings.[11]

Individuality is matter, which is an "avidity for being, having of itself no determination. . . ." In other words, individuality is potentiality, matter that can be shaped or molded. Individuality is, for example, the coloring materials that constitute the material part of an artistic work. What makes the materials beautiful is the art of the painter, the personal aspect of the painter. Individuality is a fragment, inclined to "disintegration, just as space is inclined to division."[12] Individuality is not "something bad in itself." Quite the contrary, it is good, but good only as individuality relates to the person; "what is bad is to let this aspect of our being predominate in our actions."

Maritain was clear that the person and the individual "do not represent two separate things." It is "the same entire being which, in one sense, is an individual, and, in another sense, a person." What is individual is received from matter; what is received from spirit is the person.[13] Hence, when the human being acts, it is not the person or the individual singly that is acting, it is the whole. As Aristotle explained, "to say that the soul gets angry is as if one were to say that the soul weaves or builds a house. Probably it is better not to say that the soul pities, or learns, or thinks, but to say rather that the soul is the instrument whereby man does these things."[14]

Maritain has been criticized for emphasizing the antithesis between the person and the individual while at the same time also emphasizing their apparent unity.[15] Creaveny argues that the "distinction is forced," particularly when applied to politics:

> Is not everything that pertains to man's temporal life an integral part of
> his personal totality? . . . It is precisely in this world of space and time,
> as forming part of natural society, the State, that man is divinely called
> to attain his personal salvation, and to achieve the full perfection of his
> personality.

Creaveny's argument, distilled to its essence, is that if the person is a boundary where the state cannot go [as Maritain claims] then matter, the individual, is fully subject to the caprices and whims of the state. Creaveny continues that a "Totalitarian apologist" could adopt Maritain's distinction to successfully argue that the state should have "absolute authority over the individual body! . . . The tables are turned on the Personalist . . ." and the distinction used to justify sterilization.[16]

Creaveny and those who criticize Maritain for his person-individual distinction miss the point. Sterilization, of course, does impugn the individual, the material part of the human being. It is the sexual organs that are severed in the sterilization process. But, more importantly for Maritain, sterilization also impugns the spiritual, the personal part of the human being. The degradation to the spiritual part of the person sterilized by the state is in the abridgement of the act and the right of procreation. The latter type of degradation, according to Maritain, is exactly why there should be, and there is, a distinction between person and individual, and why the distinction is valuable in analyzing the citizen's relation to the state.

Creaveny also disputes the "Thomistic patrimony" of Maritain's distinction. Thomas was ignorant of the distinction and did not oppose the person and the individual as Maritain and the other so-called "Personalists" have done.[17] Maritain, in turn, sharply criticized one of Creaveny's sources, Father Pedro Descoqs, who, Maritain said had "no difficulty" in writing a book that showed that Descoqs "did not understand the doctrine of individuality and personality."[18]

Whether or not Maritain's distinction is a true rendering of Thomas's philosophy is not relevant to a study of Maritain's political philosophy. Maritain did not slavishly follow Thomas. Instead Maritain adapted Thomistic principles to changing historical circumstances, in the case of the person-individual distinction—the rise of totalitarianism.[19] In addition to a philosophical ground, the distinction between the person and the individual had a theological ground in the doctrine of the Trinity. The theological basis is one of the important links between Christianity and democracy, as will be discussed below.

The distinction has roots that extend beyond Christianity. Maritain wrote that "There is nothing new in the distinction; it is indeed a classical distinction, belonging to the intellectual heritage of humanity. And the distinction between the '*ego*' and the '*self*' [Maritain's emphasis] in Hind[u] philosophy is—with other metaphysical connotations—its equivalent." The Hindu notion of the self is almost identical with Maritain's idea of the person as this passage from the *Satapatha Brahmana*, X.6:3 shows, "One should venerate Brahman as the True. One should venerate the Self who consists of mind . . . greater than the sky, greater than space, greater than this earth, greater than all existing things. He is the self of breath, he is my own self."[20] Western philosophers who have made the distinction include "certain disciples of Proudhon, Nicolas Berdiaeff and those philosophers who, prior to the invasion of the young existentialist group, already spoke of an 'existentialist philosophy.'"[21] Berdiaeff echoing Maritain said that the "individual is a naturalistic and sociological category. . . . Personality, on the other hand, is a spiritual and ethical category. It is not born of a father and mother, it is created spiritually and gives actual effect to the divine idea of man."[22]

Adler and Farrell criticized Maritain's distinction between the person and the individual from the viewpoint of man's temporal goal—natural happiness. *If* Maritain's distinction is valid, it naturally follows that the spiritual happiness of man is paramount even in the temporal city. "On the contrary, this natural social happiness must be spoken of, and understood, as individual because it is a perfection of the life of the complete substance of man, not of his soul. It is not the human soul which is naturally social, but man the substance composite of matter and form." Adler and Farrell argue that the individual, the material substance of man, not the spiritual, requires the "social life."[23] The rational or spiritual is "source of the peculiar administration of that need." "Personal" should only be concerned with spiritual happiness.[24]

Another critic of Maritain claimed that the distinction between the person and the individual is actually a distinction between the soul and the body, and, as such, ". . . smacks of Platonism and Cartesianism."[25] Baisnee continued that "for them [the Personalists, specifically Maritain] man is not the *compositum homanum*, but rather a soul dwelling in a body which it uses and controls when it is not overcome by it. It is true that man is a person because of his spiritual soul, but the body as well as the soul is a constitutive element of the person."[26] Baisnee said that Maritain asked the wrong questions. The real issues are what constitutes individuality and whether the person and the individual are actually opposed as Maritain maintains. Baisnee argued that Maritain's distinction is based on a misplaced concept of duty:

> We quite agree that in the hierarchy of duties man's duties to God stand above his duties to society and that God alone can claim all man's thoughts and affections, man's whole inner life. From this it follows that no totalitarian state can impose a rule of thinking on man's intelligence and a code of right living on his will. But we do not see how the distinction among duties can be made the basis of the distinction between the individual and the person. The first distinction pertains to the moral order; the other pertains to the ontological order. Because man has different duties it does not follow that he is split in two parts, the individual and the person, one of which would belong to the state, while the other would be independent of the state.[27]

Baisnee continued that Maritain's claim that individuality connotes "all tendencies that are directed by self interest: self preservation, self indulgence, selfishness and the like, while personality connotes the opposite altruistic tendencies: detachment, generosity, etc." is false. In fact, says Bainsee, Maritain has transposed the order. It is the individual because he is unique and exists in a society of unique individuals that is open to the uniqueness. Matter is malleable and accepts change. Maritain's person, however, exists for himself, "'in self defense, in resistance, and in attack.'"[28]

Baisnee and the other critics of the person-individual distinction were myopic. True, matter is malleable, it is spirituality that changes matter. It is also true that the person involves ontological duties as Baisnee claimed. However, ontology can have political implications as noted above in the discussion of the differences between Maritain's and Heidegger's ontology. Heidegger's ontology leads to a society of individuals where the spiritual is either repressed, perverted, or handed over to a Grand Inquisitor figure. Maritain conceived of the person-individual distinction as a riposte to modern totalitarianism that denigrated the person. His distinction pinpointed the critical weakness in the theoretical constructs of such regimes and belie the claims, invariably made by such regimes, that they allow their citizens complete freedom to develop their potentialities.

Moreover, Maritain's position has been vindicated by recent empirical evidence in the revolt against the totalitarian regimes in the Soviet Union and Eastern Europe. The spiritual nature of the revolt has been consistently emphasized by Czechoslovakian President Václav Havel and the other leaders of the uprising:

> The Prague Spring is usually understood as the clash between two groups on the level of real power; those who wanted to maintain the system and those who wanted to reform it. It is frequently forgotten, however, that this encounter was merely the final act and the inevitable consequence of a long drama played out chiefly in the theater of the spirit and the conscience of society.[29]

Another example is Solzhenitsyn's novels about life in the Soviet prison camps. He tells of the attempted total annihilation of the person in the camps by forcing the prisoners to be individuals in Maritain's sense. The material side of life dominated. Each day was a struggle to maintain the material needs necessary to sustain life. Yet, as Solzhenitsyn shows, it was the spiritual side of the "zeks" that enabled some men to survive and, in a certain sense, to prosper.[30] Many more examples could be given.

Adler and Farrell are correct that the whole man is concerned with the political order, a proposition with which Maritain would not disagree. They differed from Maritain on the importance of the spiritual to the political order. Maritain's political order was primarily a spiritual community grounded in a spiritual bond between citizens based on friendship and Christian charity. The political order of Maritain was required by the person, not the individual:

> To sum up: on the one hand, it is the person itself, which enters into society; and on the other hand, it is finally by reason of its material individuality that the person is in society as a part whose good is inferior to the good of the whole. If this is the case, we understand that society cannot live without the perpetual gift and the perpetual surplus which derive from persons; each *irreplaceable* [Maritain's emphasis] and incommunicable.

> We could also say that society—its life, its peace—cannot exist
> without the efficient causality of love, which is essentially personal.[31]

Only by entering into a society with other persons is the spiritual potential of each person optimally developed. That is one of the reasons why the democratic principle is intertwined with Christianity. A spiritual force, Christianity, is required to protect and vivify the spiritual, existential bond of a truly democratic society.[32]

THE PERSON AND SOCIETY

The person, "by virtue of his dignity, as well as his need, requires to be a member of society."[33] The person "requires the communication of knowledge and love. By the very fact that each of us is a person and expresses himself to himself, each of us requires communication with *other* and *the others* [Maritain's emphasis] in the order of knowledge and love. Personality . . . requires a dialogue in which souls really communicate."[34] Society, for Maritain, "is a society of persons. In so far as a city deserves this name, it is a city of human persons."[35] Persons "demand" for themselves life in society "by virtue of the very perfections which are inherent" in them, and "because of the fact of this being open to the communications of knowledge and love . . . require an entrance into relations with other persons."[36]

Spirituality for Maritain is expansive. It wants to be shared. The person has a need to share his spirituality for it is only by sharing spirituality that the person can fully develop as a person. "The human person cannot achieve fullness alone, but only through receiving certain goods essential to him from society."[37] The goods that society gives the person are the means to share his spirituality through religions associations, creative and artistic endeavors that reflect the spiritual nature of man, and a peaceful environment that will allow him to fully develop his spirituality:

> I do not mean only material needs, of bread, of clothes and lodging, for
> all of which man depends upon the aid of his fellows; but also, first of
> all, the need of their aid in acting according to reason and virtue, which
> corresponds to the specific character of the human being. In order to
> attain to a certain degree of elevation in knowledge and perfection of
> moral life, man needs the education and the aid granted by his fellows.

> . . . He is a political animal because he is a reasonable animal, because
> his reason seeks to develop with the help of education, through the
> teaching and the cooperation of other men, and because society is thus
> required to accomplish human dignity.[38]

The education Maritain refers to is not restricted to formal schooling although that is included in the term. Maritain means the education in spirituality that each person receives by uniting in an existential bond with the spirituality of the others. Each person in a society as conceived by Maritain has an opportunity to develop spirituality by formal education and by experience, observing the spirituality of fellow members of society. An analogy can be drawn with Aristotle's conception of how a moral character is developed. Aristotle tells us that moral virtue is developed by habit. The good habits are developed by education and training and "also by taking part in transactions with our fellow-men that some of us become just and others unjust. . . ."[39] Man learns moral habits then by example; by actually observing good acts being done by other people.

Maritain believed that spirituality is developed in the same way. By instruction, either formal instruction in school, or by instruction through example, such as children attending religious services with their parents. Or spirituality is developed by participating in spiritual "transactions." A spiritual "transaction" might be succoring the sick or dying, giving aid to the poor. In Maritain's democracy Christianity provides the leadership role in these spiritual "transactions." But, for Maritain, a political order is necessary before the task of developing spirituality can be undertaken.

The foregoing demonstrates that Maritain conceived that society and its political order are fundamentally spiritual in the sense that the existential bond that being, according to Maritain, forms as a result of action and reaction is, or should be, a spiritual bond. Society is also primarily spiritual because it exists to develop the spiritual nature of man. "Taken in its radical generosity," the person tends to "super-abound in social communications." Gabriel Marcel caught some of the flavor of what Maritain meant by a spiritual bond that unites society when Marcel recalled "vibrating in unison with his fellow citizens" when France entered the war against Germany in 1914. He was no longer "locked" into the narrow limits of his individuality. "We were *all together* [Marcel's emphasis]."[40] Ideally, in a political order grounded on Maritain's Christian-infused democracy, a society composed of Maritain's persons, where spiritual values are promoted, the citizens would "vibrate in unison," that is, a true community would exist. "Vibrating in unison" does not mean a conflict-free society. Nor does it mean that the citizens of such a society all love each other. It means that there is a bond, a sense of community, shared by most of citizens. In the example given by Marcel the community spirit seemingly was the result of a single event. In Maritain's democracy, the community spirit is the result of a common "moral charter" that develops over a period of time, as is more fully explained below.

INDIVIDUALITY AND THE SPIRITUAL

Individuality is bad, according to Maritain, whenever it dominates the spiritual. When that happens there is a perversion; the spiritual must dominate because the spiritual is tied to The Absolute. The practical effect of the domination of the individual over the spiritual is most pronounced in ethics or morality, which greatly influences politics, for Maritain conceived politics and economics as branches of ethics.[41]

As man moves away from the spiritual/absolute toward the material/individual man's moral compass is skewed. Man must follow "either the slope of personality or the slope of individuality."[42] No transcendent standard is accepted to control or guide human nature in the "slope of individuality." Man as individual becomes his own absolute. Again Maritain's position can be illustrated by reference to Dostoevsky, for both thinkers shared the same vision of the domination of the spiritual over the material. In *The Devils*, Dostoevsky, speaking through Stefan Verkhovensky, stated the position he and Maritain shared:

> The mere presence of the everlasting idea of the existence of something infinitely more just and happy than I, already fills me with abiding tenderness and—glory. . . . To know every moment and to believe that somewhere there exists perfect peace and happiness for everyone and for everything, is much more important to a man than his own happiness. The whole law of human existence consists merely of making it possible for every man to bow down before what is infinitely great. If man were to be deprived of the infinitely great, he would refuse to go on living, and die of despair. The infinite and the immeasurable is as necessary to man as the little planet which he inhabits.[43]

In the political order, the subjugation of the person, the spiritual, by the individual, is the hallmark of nondemocratic regimes, or of what Maritain called "anarchic" democracy. This kind of regime is identical to the former Soviet empire where spirituality is abridged by not allowing the free exercise of religion, or simply by controlling, or attempting to control, its wellsprings.[44] Maritain saw the domination of the spiritual by matter as one of the central issues for politics.

The distinction between the person and the individual was also the ground for what Maritain perceived to be the a major problem for society, the conflict between atomistic individualism and collective authoritarianism, between the rights of the person versus the rights of the community. His integral humanism, his espousal of democracy, his entire political philosophy was devoted to restoring the person to what he perceived its proper place in the political order.

> The expulsion of the element of spirit and grace from the intellectual and social life, that is to say, what is specifically human, is the secret cause of the supremacy of matter which men find so burdensome and oppressive today.
>
> This supremacy of matter must be resisted not only by the assertion of the rights of the mind and the reason, but also by the asseveration of the supremacy of divine grace and the primacy of the spiritual.[45]

Democracy, according to Maritain, is the best type of government for the comunication of spirituality and for the general domination of the spiritual over matter. In Maritain's democracy, all can fully develop their spirituality. Democracy's link with Christianity is primarily responsible for democracy's plenary position in defending spirituality. Moreover, in democracy the person has the freedom and the political equality to exercise that freedom in the political order to select a regime that will respect spirituality and provide a peaceful, noncorrupt government that will enable spirituality to flourish. In Aristotle's words "liberty and equality are chiefly to be found in democracy, . . .—with all sharing alike, as far as possible in constitutional rights—that they most likely will be found."[46]

Maritain's distinction between the person and the individual has a determining significance to his political philosophy and his theory of democracy. It was on the basis of the distinction that Maritain differentiated between two types of democracy, the democracy of the person and the democracy of the individual.

Just as the political ontology of Martin Heidegger was a window to Maritain's political ontology, by providing a glimpse of being antithetical to Maritain's, so also the study of democracy of the individual is a window to some of the critical features of Maritain's conception of democracy. There are two paramount types of individual democracy: (1) the pure Rousseauistic form that Maritain called anarchic democracy; and

(2) the liberal bourgeois form. This part of the study will focus on two common features of the defective democracies—centralization and denigration of man's spiritual nature as compared with two common features of Maritain's personalist democracy—subsidiarity and what he called the "moral charter."

INDIVIDUALITY AND DEMOCRACY

The political thinker Maritain associated with individual democracy was Jean-Jacques Rousseau. Of all the thinkers Maritain criticized none aroused his annoyance and condemnation more than Rousseau. "If we discover in ourselves, if we meet in the world, any principle that depends on Rousseauism, we shall know that this principle . . . is an old principle working itself out, that it is Christianity liquefying and rotten; and we shall throw it out, for there is nothing more absurd than to try to join and harmonize a living form and its corruption."[47]

The differences between personalist democracy and individual democracy are crystallized by the differences between Maritain and Rousseau. Their differences are fundamental—starting with being—or human nature. Maritain believed that man had a lower, evil self as a result of original sin that had to be restrained. Rousseau rejected the doctrine of original sin:

> First, it is far from being the case, according to me, that this doctrine of original sin, subject to such terrible difficulties, is contained in Scripture either as clearly or as harshly as it has pleased Augustine the Rhetorician and our Theologians to erect it; and how can one conceive that God creates so many innocent and pure souls, expressly for the purpose of joining them to sinful bodies in order to make them contract moral corruption there and in order to condemn them all to hell for no other crime than this union which is his work.[48]

Rousseau's denial of original sin was consistent with his conception of human nature—man is inherently good. Virtue was an inherent characteristic of human nature. He said, "O virtue! Sublime science of simple souls are not your principles engraved in all hearts, and is it not enough in order to learn your laws, to return into oneself and in the silence of the passions to listen to the voice of one's conscience."[49] Virtue is found in the "simple souls," e.g., prepolitical man, man in a state of nature. Human beings are corrupted by society which makes man weak, "timorous, groveling."[50] Virtue is lost in political society unless the type of political society conforms as nearly as possible to Rousseau's state of nature.

Rousseau's reference to the "silence of the passions" is also important for he conceived man as an animal, a "human machine,"[51] ruled by passion. In Rousseau's words, "human understanding owes much to the Passions which, as is commonly admitted, also owes much to it."[52] Virtue is perfected through the passions which imbue man with a desire to know. Without this desire virtue would be sterile.

From Rousseau's concept of virtue flow political and social concepts which, in turn, are actualized in political and social institutions. Since man is inherently good and is only corrupted by organized society, the ideal political society is that which, as nearly as possible, restores man to the original state of nature where his inherent goodness, sparked by compassion, will enable man to live in harmony with his fellow human beings. A leitmotif which permeates Rousseauistic political thinking then is that society is the cause of human misery; the Archimedean objective of the political system is to make all happy by changing society.

Society is harmful, destructive. Men leave the state of nature where they are truly happy out of self-preservation, not out of an inherent desire to communicate, to share spirituality. Man is corrupted by society. Man reaches perfection only by returning to a Rousseauistic state of nature. Only then can man know and understand himself:

> Buried in the forest, I looked for and found there the image of the first times, of which I proudly traced the history; I demolished the little lies of men, I dared to unveil their nature in its nakedness, to follow the progress of the times and the things that have disfigured it and comparing the man of man [man in society] with natural man, to show him in his alleged perfection the actual source of his miseries.[53]

Rousseau described savage man as one who "breathes nothing but repose and freedom; he wants only to live and remain idle." Civilized man is "always active, sweats, scurries, constantly agonizes in search of still more strenuous occupations, he works to the death, even rushes toward it in order to be in a position to live, or renounces life in order to acquire immortality."[54]

On the other hand, Maritain believed that society was natural and necessary, formed by a spiritual bond between beings who are persons. The person must have a society in order to develop his spirituality. The person must act and react with other human beings. Society is necessary. Maritain called Rousseauistic democracy "nonsensical," a "spurious democratic" philosophy, and:[55]

> Democracy, conceived in the manner of Rousseau, *suppresses authority and preserves power*. It is this type of Democracy which for almost two centuries now has prevailed in the ideology of Western peoples. One may call it liberal or bourgeois democracy, or masked anarchic democracy. Its root proper is in the following principle: since each individual, as Rousseau tells us, is "born free" (it is clear that each individual is born endowed with *free will*, but it is evidently not the latter which interests Rousseau; he is equivocal as to the word "free," and means a certain kind of existence, *a freedom of independence),*—since every individual is born free, his dignity demands that he *should obey only himself*. Naturally . . . the dialectic of this democracy leads to the formula of the *Social Contract*; "to find a form of association . . . through which every man united with all others, should nevertheless obey only himself and remain as free as before [all emphases are Maritain's]".[56]

The many in the pure form of individual, anarchic democracy in theory rule. In practice, however, the many surrender their political will to a "common conscience" or general will that exercises total control over the political order. The power of the many acting through their common conscience is supreme so that a totalitarian political order results although ostensibly democratic in form.[57] This type of democracy is "blind to the realities of the spirit . . . they perceive in man only the shadow of real personality—the material individuality." Later on it will be shown that Tocqueville and Maritain saw that the inherent materiality that is most pronounced in Rousseau's anarchic democracy is endemic to democracy in general. There must be a spiritual force to combat this inherent tendency in democracy. For Maritain and Tocqueville, the only force capable of restraining materiality in democracy is religion—specifically Christianity.

Anarchic democracy does not, it cannot, recognize the independence, the wholeness of the person, because its independence is a particularity, a particular will in Rousseau's terms, that refuses total assimilation into the absolute unity of the general will. Maritain clearly saw the danger to the spiritual posed by the exercise of unbridled power in the name of the many. By concentrating on the individual, anarchic democracy tends to "deteriorate, to vilify and to enslave the person, either by dissolving it in anarchy, or as inevitably happens under the natural necessities of political life, by submitting it entirely to the social body as Number, as Economic Community, or as the State."[58] The French Revolution is the paradigm of an anarchic democracy's complete subjugation of the person to the state. Louis Saint-Just, Robespierre's compatriot, told the National Convention, for example, that "there is something terrifying in the sacred love of one's country. It is so all exclusive that it sacrifices everything, without pity, without fear, without regard for humanity, to the public interest. . . . You cannot make a republic with compromises, but only with ruthless severity, but is the expression of their common political will."[59] Robespierre's "intellectual and emotional debt to Rousseau is complex and profound."[60] Robespierre called Rousseau "the teacher of the human race. If only he had been witness to this Revolution of which he was the precursor, and which has carried him to the Pantheon, who can doubt his generous soul would have embraced with transport the cause of justice and equality."[61]

Anarchic democracy can be analyzed in terms of the one and the many. The general will emerges from a concurrence between the many and the one. In the anarchic democracy there is a many, the citizens of the anarchic democracy. The many ones concur to produce a one in the general will in which all the many ones are completely merged, although the one is distinct from the many.[62] Maritain described the concurrence when he referred to the general will as a "myth" that leads to a "totalitarian dictatorship," where the "entire sovereign multitude is reabsorbed in the unique person of a half-god sprung forth from the multitude."[63]

NOTES

1. The term "personalist" derives from Maritain's conception of the person, which Maritain claimed has Thomistic roots, a claim disputed by some Thomists. See below. In *The Peasant of the Garonne*, 51-52, Maritain claimed that "personalist" and "communitarian" had become

> something of a catch phrase for French Catholic thought. . . . At a time
> when it mattered very much to oppose to the totalitarian slogans a
> new—and true—one, I had greatly solicited my gray cells, and finally
> in one of my books of that period advanced the phrase in question. It
> was from me that Mounier got it. The expression is right, but when I
> see the way it is now being used, I am not very proud of it. For it is
> clear that after paying lipservice to the "personalist," it is really the
> "communitarian" which those who use it now cherish.

See also Emmanuel Mounier, *Personalism*, trans. Philip Maret (Notre Dame, Indiana: University of Notre Dame Press, n.d.).

2. *Scholasticism and Politics*, 65.

3. Ibid., 62.

4. Ibid.

5. Ibid., 63.

6. Ibid.

7. Ibid.

8. *Integral Humanism*, 9.

9. *Scholasticism and Politics*, 64.

10. Ibid., 61.

11. Jacques Maritain, *The Person and the Common Good*, translated, John J. FitzGerald (Notre Dame, Indiana: University of Notre Dame Press, 1966), 34.

12. Ibid., 38.

13. *Scholasticism and Politics*, 65.

14. Aristotle, *De Anima*, Book A, chap. 4, 408b11-15.

15. John A. Creaveny, "Person and Individual," *The New Schoolman*, vol. XVII, no. 3 (July, 1943), 231.

16. Ibid., 248.

17. Ibid., 245.

18. *Scholasticism and Politics*, 61.

19. *Maritain on the Nature of Man in a Christian Democracy*, 15-16.

20. Ibid., 58-59. R. C. Zaehner, *Hinduism* (London: n.p., 1962), 66. Brahman is the ultimate reality with which the self is identified.

21. *The Person and the Common Good*, 34.

22. Nicolas Berdiaeff, *The Beginning and the End*, translated, R. M. French (New York: Harper & Brothers, 1953), 135-136.

23. *The Thomist* 4: 178.

24. Ibid.

25. Jules A. Baisnee, "Two Catholic Critiques of Personalism," *The Modern Schoolman*, vol. XXII, No. 2 (January, 1945): 59, 65.

26. Ibid.

27. Ibid., 67.

28. Ibid., 67-68. Baisnee cited Father Descoqs. The attack on Maritain prompted a reply. See, for example, I. Thomas Eschmann, "In Defense of Jacques Maritain," *The Modern Schoolman*, vol. XXII, no. 4 (May, 1945), 183.

29. Václav Havel, et al., *The Power of the Powerless*, intro. Steven Lukes (Armonk, New York: Palach Press, 1985), 43.

30. Aleksandr Solzhenitsyn, *One Day in the Life of Ivan Denisovich*, trans. Ralph Parker (New York: New American Library, 1963).

31. *Scholasticism and Politics*, 76-77.

32. *Christianity and Democracy*, 50-51.

33. *Scholasticism and Politics*, 67. Maritain does not define what he means by "society." Nor does he differentiate between "society" and the political order or the political community so that the terms are used interchangeably.

34. *The Person and the Common Good*, 42.

35. *Scholasticism and Politics*, 67.

36. Ibid., 68.

37. Ibid., 68.

38. Ibid.

39. Aristotle, *Nichomachean Ethics*, bk. II, ch. i.

40. Gabriel Marcel, "Reply to John E. Smith," trans. Dr. Girard Etzkorn, *The Philosophy of Gabriel Marcel*, ed. Paul Arthur Schlipp and Lewis Edwin Hahn, Library of Living Philosophers, vol. XVII (La Salle, Illinois: Open Court, 1991), 350. The relationship between Maritain and Marcel has not been fully explored. Both were French intellectuals who converted to Catholicism, scions of wealthy families. Marcel was an occasional visitor to Jacques and Raïssa Maritain's Thomistic study groups in the pre-World War II years. At one time, Marcel, accompanied by Charles Du Bos, attended weekly meetings with Jacques Maritain "who took great pains to help us understand Thomistic thought better and to appreciate it more. All three of us showed good will but the result was meager indeed." Gabriel Marcel, "An Autobiographical Essay," *The Philosophy of Gabriel Marcel*, 30.

There apparently was an underlying tension between Maritain and Marcel. In either 1937 or 1938, Marcel refused to sign a petition circulated in Paris by "Jacques Maritain and his friends" to protest political conditions in Austria. Marcel refused to sign out of fear of undermining Chancellor Dolfus's opposition to Hitler. Ibid., 36.

In 1934, in a review of Maritain's *Degrees of Knowledge* in *Revue des jeunes*, Marcel "ventured to express the idea" that Maritain's attachment to scholastic terminology "risked rendering a disservice to Christianity by supporting the notion that it remained bound to a medieval mode of thought and thus seemed unable to accommodate the conquests of science and modern philosophy." Maritain was hurt by the review. He asked Marcel, "or saw to it that I was asked—not to publish the article. I assented with a smile." Ibid., 30-31.

See H. Stuart Hughes, "Marcel, Maritain and the Secular World," *The American Scholar*, vol. 35 (Autumn, 1966): 728 and Bernard E. Doering, *Jacques Maritain and the French Catholic Intellectuals*, 73, 77, 81, 94, 252, 254. Hughes says that "from the start" Maritain and Marcel lived in a "different mental universe. Marcel saw in words and reasoning no more than the external trappings of the mysteries of being." Hughes implies that Maritain saw being as primarily speculative and theoretical. This study challenges Hughes's analysis. Maritain's being is being in action. His being as subjectivity, while the predicate for spirituality, is anything but theoretical supplying with being as action a ground for a practical political order.

Maritain characterized Marcel's "approach to metaphysical being in the deepening of the sense of certain moral realities such as fidelity . . . so that the notion of fidelity is here understood in a sense which ought to transcend ethics and convey to us a strictly metaphysical value and content." Maritain believed that Marcel's being as fidelity had value, but the concept did not probe the intuition of being sufficiently. Jacques Maritain, "The Intuition of Being," *Challenges and Renewals*, ed. Joseph W. Evans and Leo R. Ward (Notre Dame, Indiana: University of Notre Dame Press, 1968), 125.

41. See Jacques Maritain, "Religion and Culture," Jacques Maritain, Peter Wust, Christopher Dawson, *Essays on Order*, general introduction, Christopher Dawson, general editors, Christopher Dawson and J. F. Burns (New York: The Macmillan Company, 1931), 26.

42. *Scholasticism and Politics*, 65.

43. Fyodor Dostoevsky, *The Devils*, trans. and introduction, David Magarshack (New York: Penguin Books, 1953) Part 3, Chapter 7, 3 at 657.

44. See, i.e., Czeslaw Milosz, *The Captive Mind*, trans. Jane Zielonko (New York: Vintage Books, 1955).

45. Jacques Maritain, *The Things That Are Not Caesar's*, trans. J. F. Scanlan (New York: Charles Scribner's, 1931). See Introduction.

46. *Politics*, bk. IV, ch. iv.

47. Jacques Maritain, *Three Reformers* (London: Sheed and Ward, 1950), 147.

48. Jean-Jacques Rousseau, *Letter to Christopher de Beaumont* in Rousseau, *Complete Works*, vol. 4, pp. 937-938.

49. Jean-Jacques Rousseau, *Discourse on the Science and Arts*, Part II, § 61. trans. and ed. Victor Gourevitch, Perennial Library (New York: Harper And Row, 1986), 27.

50. *Discourse On The Origin and the Foundations Of Inequality Among Men*, Part I, § 11.

51. Ibid.

52. Ibid., § 18.

53. Jean Jacques Rousseau, *Complete Works*, ed. Bernard Gagnebin and Marcel Raymone, vol. I, *The Confessions* (Paris: Gallimard, 1969) bk. 8, p. 388 as translated in Ann Hartle, *The Modern Self in Rousseau's Confessions*, Revisions Series, general editors, Stanley Hauerwas and Alasdair MacIntyre (Notre Dame, Indiana: University of Notre Dame Press, 1983), 135.

54. *Discourse on the Origin and the Foundations of Inequality Among Men*, Part 2, 57.

55. *Man and the State*, 44-48. See also, *inter alia*, *The Three Reformers*, 126-140.

56. Ibid., 94. Maritain is quoting *The Social Contract*, bk. I, ch. VI.

57. *Scholasticism and Politics*, 95.

58. Ibid., 78.

59. See Louis-Antoine Saint-Just, "To The Convention, for the Committee of Public Safety demanding the Heads of Danton and Others, March, 1794," in *Liberty or Death*, ed. Denis Roche (Paris: Tchou, 1969), 49.

60. David P. Jordan, *The Revolutionary Career of Maximilien Robespierre* (New York: The Free Press, 1985), 32-33.

61. Maximillien Robespierre, *Complete Works*, X, 455.

62. See Paul Weiss, *Modes of Being* (Carbondale, Illinois: Southern Illinois University Press, 1968) 503-504. Weiss speculated that the concurrence analysis of the one and the many could be applied to the state as conceived by Thomas Hobbes. I think that it can also be fruitful in analyzing a Rousseauistic type of democracy.

63. *Scholasticism and Politics*, 94-95.

CHAPTER 4

THE BOURGEOIS LIBERAL AND PERSONALIST DEMOCRACIES

Another form of individual democracy, according to Maritain, is what he called bourgeois liberalism, which is grounded on the individual, "on his caprice, on the absolute liberty of property, of commerce and of the pleasures of life," leading eventually to the primacy of the state.[1] In the bourgeois liberal state the individual is free to do as he pleases, he has only to obey himself, as Rousseau said. In this form, individual democracy does not have a general will imposing absolute unity on its citizens. In terms of the one and the many, the many are not reabsorbed into the one as in the anarchic democracy. The many not only retain their individuality, but their individuality controls the one, the state, which mediates between the many ones. Invariably, the many in a paradoxical twist, lose their control because the state in order to function in its role of mediator must establish an instrument to execute its mediating authority, the bureaucracy. The end result is that "the individual will find himself entirely subjected to the social whole by the mechanical connections which insure his junction with it. No doubt his freedom will remain full and complete, but in an illusory mode and in the world of dreams."[2]

Maritain saw consumerism, materialism, and anthropocentric humanism as the lodestars of this political order, it is like "barren wheat and starchy bread."[3]

Barren and starchy because it lacks a "common faith which could enable it to resist disintegration." Society is broken into atomistic individuals, each independent of the other. This type of democracy lacks the existential, spiritual bond that for Maritain was vital for the creation of a true community. There is little of the communication with which the person superabounds. A genuine democracy implies a "fundamental agreement between minds and wills on the bases of life in common; it is aware of itself and of its principles, and it must be capable of defending and promoting its own conception of social and political life; it must bear within itself a common human creed, the creed of freedom."

The bourgeois liberal type of democracy is "a kind of lists or arena in which all the conceptions of the bases of common life, even those most destructive to freedom and law" are met with indifference. Bourgeois liberalism has "no brains of its own, but a neutral, empty skull clad with mirrors."[4]

Maritain is not referring to a religious creed when he talks of "common human creed." While his personalist democracy is Christian-inspired, bourgeois liberalism lacks even the minimum spiritual core that is set off from the spirituality of religious belief. This minimum spiritual core "deals with practical tenets which the human mind can try to justify from quite different philosophical [not theological] outlooks, probably because they depend basically on simple, 'natural' apperceptions" which constitute the human conscience. There are two levels of spirituality that form the existential bond of society for Maritain. First, there is a minimum level, different from the spirituality of Christianity. Then there is a higher level attained when the democracy is Christian-inspired.

Maritain's conception of democracy can be conceived as a continuum. At its lowest point is individual democracy, which is a "bad" democracy. In the middle of the line is personalist democracy, a regime without Christianity. It is a "good" type of democracy, but not the "best." Personalist democracy inspired by Christianity is the best. In fact, even the middle-level democracy is Christian-inspired in the sense that it has "been awakened by the Gospel leaven fermenting in the obscure depths of human history." This minimum level of spirituality is present when men of diverse theological and philosophical beliefs "revere . . . truth, intelligence, human dignity, freedom, brotherly love, and the absolute value of moral good."[5]

THE MORAL CHARTER

Maritain argued that the "body politic" has a right and a duty to promote through education the practical tenets that comprise the "national communion and civil peace of society." The body politic "has no right," however, to impose on its citizens a specified philosophical or theological creed "which would present itself as the only possible justification of the practical charter. . . ." Maritain asks rhetorically what would the be the content of the moral charter that comprises the national communion? He answers that it would comprise the following:

> rights and liberties of the human person, political rights and liberties, social rights and social liberties, corresponding responsibilities; rights and duties of members who are a part of family society; and liberties and obligations of the latter toward the body politic, natural rights and duties of groups and the State; government of the people, by the people and for the people; functions of authority in a political and social democracy, moral obligations binding in conscience, regarding just laws as well as the Constitution which guarantees the peoples' liberties; exclusion of the resort to coups (*coups d'etat*) in a society that is truly free and ruled by laws whose change and evolution depend on the popular majority; human equality, justice between persons and the body politic; justice between the body politic and persons, civil friendship and an ideal of fraternity, religious freedom, mutual tolerance and mutual respect between various spiritual communities and schools of thought, civic self-devotion and love of the motherland, reverence for its history and heritage, and understanding the various traditions that combine to create its unity; obligations of each person toward the common good of the body politic and obligations of each nation toward the common good of civilized society, and the necessity of becoming aware of the unity of the world and of the existence of a community of peoples.[6]

MARITAIN'S HISTORICISM

Maritain opined that the people of the United States and France who have had historical experience with the vicissitudes of democracy in their struggles for freedom, would almost universally accept the moral charter that he has laid out above.[7] His comment is warrant to briefly interject a discussion of Maritain's historicism. He believed that culture is shaped by historical circumstances. The "spirit" of the particular culture flows from the social elements of the society that predominately direct what shape the culture and the body politic created by the culture will take.[8] The most important social element for Maritain is the spiritual element, but that element is conditioned by historical circumstances. For example, during the Middle Ages, the person was recognized, but in a special way. A psychology was developed from the point of view of God so that "the gaze of mediaeval man turned away from himself."[9] Hence, there developed a political order that was hierarchical and that was subordinated to the spiritual.

Maritain's historicism is value-centered. That is, he believed that history reveals how universal ethical and moral standards, the standards of Christianity, have been applied in concrete historical settings. "A number of factual data are accumulated by history, and now from these data concerning a period of history or any other aspect of history some universal objects of thought are universally abstracted by the philosopher."[10] His value-centered historicism is in contrast to the school of political thinkers led by Leo Strauss who equate historicism with relativism.[11]

Maritain addressed the issue of historical relativism in *Integral Humanism*. He identified two "opposed errors" in a philosophy of culture. Equivocity holds that "with a change in time historical conditions become so different that they depend on supreme rules which are themselves heterogeneous: as though truth and right, the supreme rules of human action, were mutable." On the other hand a philosophy of univocity "would have us believe that these supreme rules and principles always apply in the same way, and . . . Christian principles are proportioned to the conditions of each age and are realized in time should not vary at all."[12]

Maritain's position is a philosophy of analogy. True principles and the "supreme practical rules of human life" do not change. But they are "applied in ways essentially diverse, ways answering the same concept only according to a similitude of proportion." Maritain's position presupposes a "truly rational and philosophical notion of the diverse phases of history," while equivocity and univocity are products of historical "opportunism."[13] Maritain's historicism has implications for his political philosophy for democracy can develop in historical stages; the specific type of democracy is conditioned by the historical era in which a society finds itself at any particular time. For example, from his comments regarding the acceptance of his proposed moral charter by the United States and France, Maritain thought that the two countries had arrived at his mid level personalist democracy. Their advancement to his Christian-inspired democracy would be partly dependent on the historical circumstances in both countries that developed after World War II.

THE DEFENSE OF THE MORAL CHARTER

In addition to being a list of practical tenets in which citizens of the midlevel personalist democracy should be educated, the foregoing also serves as a political agenda for that type democracy and for the more advanced Christian-inspired democracy. It is noteworthy that it is the "body politic" not the state that has a duty to promote and defend the practical tenets of the moral charter. Maritain saw this duty as a responsibility of the culture. His reliance on the culture is important for Maritain was keenly aware that historical circumstances had changed. He knew that his personalist or Christian-inspired democracy would not have the power or the support of the temporal authority that Christianity had in the Middle Ages.

He also knew that culture rather than political institutions was the instrument through which his Christian-inspired democracy would be transmitted to a political order. In this he agreed with Tocqueville. He differentiated between the state and the "body politic." The "body politic" includes all of the constituent elements of what Maritain called the "national community," which is the sum total of the subsidiary organizations, the family, local associations, etc. that make up the body politic.[14]

The duty to defend the moral charter is significant. Maritain was opposed to the freewheeling, anything goes society that is the hallmark of modern liberalism and its concomitant bourgeois liberal society and culture. He recognized that the midlevel personalist democracy could fall back into bourgeois liberal democracy, or even anarchic democracy at any time. He advocated vigorous measures to prevent such a retreat:

> Here if we want to be thorough in our thought and do not fear words, we should point out that where faith is—divine or human—there are also heretics who threaten the unity of the community, either religious or civil. In the "sacral" society the heretic was the breaker of religious unity. In the lay society of free men the heretic is the breaker of the "common democratic beliefs and practices," the totalitarian, the one who denies freedom—his neighbor's freedom—and the dignity of the human person, and the moral power of law. We do not wish him to be burned, or expelled from the city, or outlawed, or put in a concentration camp. But the democratic community should defend itself against him, by keeping him out of its leadership, through a strong and informed public opinion, even handing him over to justice when his activity endangers the security of the state—and over and above all by strengthening everywhere a philosophy of life, intellectual conviction and constructive work which would make his influence powerless.[15]

Maritain did not specify what measures the "body politic" could take to silence those he called "political heretics."[16] Here is another example of his value-centered historicism. The "lessons of history" teach that a "democratic society should not be an unarmed society, which the enemies of liberty may calmly lead to the slaughterhouse in the name of liberty." One of the values that history has taught that Maritain accepts as having universal validity is that a democratic regime has the right of self-defense.[17] Democracy must defend the moral charter that forms the body politic's nucleus "with particular energy against those who, out of principle refuse to accept, and who even work to destroy, the foundations of common life. . . ."[18]

FREEDOM OF EXPRESSION

What actions did Maritain consider permissible for a democracy to take to defend itself against the political heretic? The first line of defense is not the state, but the community. When the political heretic engages in political activity, "he shall be met with, and checked by, opposite political activity freely developed by citizens in a body politic sufficiently lively and alive."[19] The political heretic and his followers constitute a faction as defined by James Madison in *Federalist* 10. The activities of the political heretic are "adverse to the rights of the other citizens," and to "the permanent and aggregate interests of the community." By opposing the political heretic with the body politic, Maritain endorsed Madison's concept of pitting faction against faction,[20] although the two thinkers differed on the effect of religion on factions. Maritain's ideal body politic would be imbued with a Christian spirit that would rein in self-interest. Madison said that it was well known that "neither moral or religious motives can be relied on as an adequate control" of factions.[21]

Maritain and Madison agreed that factions cannot be controlled in an anarchic democracy. In the nonanarchic democracy, Madison relied on the extended sphere and representation to inhibit factions. While Maritain also saw representative government as a moderating influence on the body politic, he believed that the best defense was the body politic itself, "with the sense of community it normally entails, [the body politic] has at its disposal the spontaneous pressure of the common consciousness and public opinion, which spring from the national ethos when it is firmly established, and which are strong enough to keep political heretics out of leadership."[22]

When the political heretic engages in illegal political activity the harm to the body politic is potentially greater warranting the involvement of the

State's coercive power. In situations of this kind, the political heretic is to be handed "over to Justice," the judicial power of the State.[23]

The most vexatious class of political heretics for a democracy to attend to are those who misuse the right of free expression, one of the basic rights of Maritain's person, as will be discussed below. The "difficulty begins" when it comes to freedom of expression, "the speaking and writing activities of the political heretic."[24] Historical precedent is a guide to dealing with this problem:

> So great is the confusion today [1951] that we see common sense principles which have been ignored in the past by the worshippers of a false and deceiving liberty, being now used in false and deceiving manner in order to destroy true liberty. Those maxims—dealing with our obligations toward objective truth and with the rights of the common good—which were branded as an outrage against human autonomy when the Catholic Church set them forth to condemn theological liberalism, and which, by opposing unbridled, divinely unlimited freedom of expression, were of a nature to save freedom of expression—the Communist State is now trumpeting them and perverting them in order to simply annihilate freedom of expression. A sad Time. And, for everybody, an opportunity for melancholy reflections.[25]

What are these maxims? First, "it is not true that every thought, as such, because of the mere fact that it was born in the human intellect, has the right to be spread about in the body politic."[26] Maritain conceded that censorship, "police methods," and any "direct restriction" on freedom of expression are the "worst way" for a democracy to defend itself.[27] But those methods are acceptable in "certain cases of necessity." Maritain did not elaborate. He apparently accepted the idea that free expression is not an absolute right. This is an important concession for his body politic is comprised of persons who have an inherent desire to communicate. However, in some circumstances this natural inclination must be abridged. Exactly what those circumstances are cannot be stated with certainty due to the range of situations that could confront a democracy in the practical world.

An implication, nonetheless, can be drawn from Maritain's writings that his position was similar to the position of Justice Oliver Wendell Holmes, Jr., who fashioned the "clear and present danger test" for the United States Supreme Court as a morning star for determining the limits of free expression:

> We admit that in many places and ordinary times, the defendants in
> saying all that was said in the circular would have been within their
> constitutional rights. But the character of every act depends upon the
> circumstances in which it is done. . . . The question in every case is
> whether the words are used in such circumstances and are of such a
> nature as to create a clear and present danger that they will bring about
> the substantive evils that Congress has a right to prevent. It is a
> question of proximity and degree. When a nation is at war many things
> that might be said in time of peace are such a hindrance to its effort that
> their utterance will not be endured.[28]

The "clear and present danger test" is grounded on a speech-action distinction; "'Expression must be freely allowed and encouraged. 'Action' can be controlled. . . .'"[29] Maritain accepted Holmes's dichotomy between speech and action. When the political heretic threatens the "democratic charter by tangible acts he undertakes or by receiving money from a foreign State to subsidize antidemocratic propaganda," his right to free expression can be abridged.[30] In *The Responsibility of an Artist*, Maritain reiterated "When it comes to the *moral* or *immoral* value of a literary work, the community may have to guard its standards against it to the extent that it is an *incitation to action*. . . . We cannot deny that people who are not specialists in literature have a right to be warned against reading authors whose artistic talent is but a means to unburden their vices and obsessions on us [Maritain's emphases]."[31]

By "tangible acts he undertakes," the political heretic has crossed the boundary that separates expression from action, suppression from freedom to speak. When the survival of the democracy requires, freedom of expression can be truncated for the common good. In these instances the natural desire for communication inherent in the person must yield to the overriding good of the body politic.

Maritain's second maxim was that State interference was to be "practical, not ideological: the more extraneous this criterion is to the very content of thought the better it will be." In addition to its applicability in the purely political arena, the second maxim operates in free expression situations concerning obscenity. Maritain certainly considered obscenity to be a form of political heresy, it undermines the moral charter of the democracy. He thought the state incapable of exercising aesthetic judgment, "it would condemn Baudelaire or Joyce." He preferred that the State interfere in the business aspects of obscenity. The critical issue is whether the author or publisher "plans" to profit from the work.[32] Maritain did not say so, but it can be implied from this passage that he favored prior restraint to prevent the distribution of obscene material. If the plan is to make money then State intervention was permissible in the form of judicial action either to seize the offending material, or to seize whatever profits might accrue from the sale of the offending material, before the material is actually distributed to the public.

Maritain joined the pornographers with a third group of political heretics that he considered the most dangerous to a democratic body politic—"intellectual corrupters of the human mind."[33] He did not identify who comprised this group. For this last group Maritain rejected State intervention because intelligence was required to combat this group and the state is "not equipped to deal with matters of intelligence," only a spiritual body—the Church—is so equipped.

The intellectual corrupters would be combated by an informed public opinion led by a "special body" of citizens whose moral and intellectual integrity was beyond reproach.[34] Who these citizens are or how they were to be selected he did not specify. His writings in this area were sparse, filled with lacunae. His proposals for combating obscenity were also not fully developed. Flesh can be added to the bones of his thought about censorship by looking to the thought of his intellectual soulmate, John Courtney Murray, S.J., on the American experience with censorship.

Murray and Maritain agreed on basic principles: that every government has the right of self-defense, that this right extends to public morals, what Maritain would call the moral charter of society, that public opinion is the best defense of a democratic society against abuses of free expression, that government interference in this area should be kept to a minimum, and that procedural fairness and rule of law must be involved in any state action.[35] Given the two thinkers' convergence on the essentials, Murray's comments on censorship provide an insight into Maritain's rationale for limiting free expression to defend democracy's moral charter.

Murray offered two grounds for minimum state intervention in free expression. First, that "social freedom is a complex, whose constituent elements are closely interlocked. You may . . . wish to 'clean up' political campaigns by limiting the freedom of the contestants to attack each other's personal integrity; but the means you take . . . may damage the freedom of the electoral process itself."[36] Second, that state or institutional interference is generally ineffective. Witness, for example, the futile attempt to control sexual activity by the Catholic Church through restraints on free expression. In 1592, when the Church's Index of Forbidden Books was "being used with extreme severity" there were more than 9,000 prostitutes in a total population of 70,000 in Rome, at that time the capital of the Papal States. In 1517, the number of prostitutes in Rome outnumbered the number of married women.[37]

Murray agreed with Maritain that special groups should lead the defense of the body politic against obscenity. "Coercion of a more informal kind—through economic pressure, etc.—is also employed by various associations, that do not hesitate to identify themselves as 'power-groups.' Such, for instance is a trade union."[38] The "power-group" might boycott a motion picture, for example. Murray would allow the people a limited right to define obscenity. "The people, in general, have a fairly clear notion of what obscenity is. They should be able to decide at least for themselves and for their families." However, the "ordinary father and mother" is not qualified to act as censor for the society at large, "or to decide what literature or movies may be displayed before the general public."[39] The interests of the family might not be the same as the interests of the body politic for the latter has an abiding interest in free expression that the family does not have. "If therefore any censorship is to be administered in the interest of society, the professional competence of the literary critic must play a role in the process."[40]

When the state is involved, Murray opined:

> In one further and final respect the process of extralegal censorship ought to be juridical, pursued in the spirit of law—that is, in its adoption of minimal aims. Fussiness is out of order. There ought to be a few, only a few, areas of concentration, in which a little bit (if not much) can be done. I suggest that the chief area is the "pornography of violence," as it has been called. Mischief enough is done by the obscenities that occur in the portrayal of illicit love (by literary hacks who never learned what the genuine artist knows instinctively—that, though art may "say all," there are certain things that it is never allowed to say explicitly).[41]

Murray's comments are consistent with Maritain's concept of government of, by, and for the people. It would be appropriate in Maritain's democracy, whether midlevel personalist or Christian-inspired, for the people, who are persons in various stages of development, to exercise their right of self-determination in this area of their lives also. The people do this by enlarging the spiritual bond of the body politic by acting as a restraining force through public opinion and private morality, the latter are part of the "spiritual transactions" discussed above. The people also exercise plenary power over the contents of the moral charter through their control of the government.

Maritain wrote that in democracy the legislative power "must be exercised" by the peoples' representatives and the executive power by officials appointed by the people, either directly or indirectly, or controlled by the people.[42] To summarize, in the area of obscenity and of political heresy generally the people would "rule" in three ways: (1) directly—in their own families; (2) indirectly—through public opinion and their private acts that are observed by the public; and (3) indirectly—through their representatives in the legislature or through the executive branch.

In dealing with the intellectual corrupter and the purveyor of obscenity Maritain's reliance on public morality was another example of his belief that the person, the spiritual side of man, must dominate a body politic. Public morality is a reflection of the collective spirituality of each person. To Maritain, the spirituality of many persons when combined in public opinion and public morality will be greater than the spirituality of any one person. He borrowed from Aristotle who acknowledged that if there is a body of good men who are at the same time good citizens, they will be better, less corrupt or corruptible, than the one good man.[43] Therefore, for Maritain, the people rule not only in the political order, but also in the social sphere. "[D]emocracy is the regime wherein the people enjoy their social and political majority and exercise it to conduct their own affairs."[44] Socially, the people "rule" by establishing the moral and ethical values of a society so that those values are not imposed from above as has been historically done by a noble or gentry class.

CULTURE AND THE MORAL CHARTER

The moral charter that Maritain thought was a necessity for a personalist democracy must have the concurrence of the people if the spiritual bond is to develop. Hence, the people have a voice in the moral values that vivify the charter. The people rule politically and socially. This does not mean that the body politic's ethical and moral values should be formed by the masses in a manner similar to the creation of the materialistic, sexually explicit, consumer-oriented "pop culture" of the present day United States and Europe. Pop culture for Maritain would be a morally corrupt culture. He would apply his criticism of several Russian and German philosophers' material and mechanistic conception of culture to today's pop culture. Pop culture is a creation of avant garde elements in the entertainment and music industries. Just as Maritain rejected the cultural values of the dissolute gentry class so he would also reject the values of an entertainment and music industry saturated with materialistic ideas of what is the good life.

His argument for the social rule of the people is based on a belief in what might be called a "Christian yeoman" person, the stable, hard-working, morally driven, individuals that comprise the working class. His position on cultural values as a political force can be likened to the position of the Antifederalists during the ratification debates over the Constitution, when cultural values was one of the central issues, although the debate was framed in the language of political representation.

The Antifederalists feared that the system of representation of the proposed Constitution would result in an aristocratic government in which the "common man" would have little say. One of the leading Antifederalists, Melancton Smith, for example, opined that few of the "middling class" would run for Congress because of the high lifestyle that representatives would adopt. Congress was not a place where the "sensible, substantial men, who have been used to walking in the plain and frugal paths of life" would feel comfortable. "A substantial yeoman, of sense and discernment, will hardly ever be chosen."[45]

Like the Antifederalists, Maritain had faith in those who walk in the "plain and frugal paths of life." "The first axiom and precept in democracy is to trust the people. Trust the people, respect the people, trust them even and first of all while awakening them, that is, while putting yourself at the service of their human dignity."[46]

Who are the many or the people? Maritain said that they can be defined negatively as the mass of the nonprivileged. He preferred a positive definition, "that moral community which is centered on manual labor (allowing for the imprecision that such a description entails)—a moral community made up of the bulk of those who labor with their hands, farmers and workers, and also of the various elements which in point of fact are socially and morally bound up with them."[47]

Maritain identified the people with a certain "historical patrimony connected with labor, and made up of sorrows, efforts, and hopes," as well as a certain "inner moral behavior," a consciousness, a certain way of understanding and "living out suffering, poverty, hardship, and especially work itself, a certain conception of how a man must help or correct another," that includes belonging to the "anonymous mass. . . ."[48] In a nutshell, the people, according to Maritain, are the working class, the "common" human beings who constitute the majority of humankind. They are not the intelligentsia or the gentry, nor are the many the noble class of Aristotle and Plato, the aristocratic few. The many for Maritain are also not the poor. So he and Aristotle differ, for Aristotle said that democracy is when the "free, who are also poor and the majority govern."[49]

Maritain's many are those primarily in the middle and lower middle class. This group, according to Maritain, have a historical tie with Christianity. Maritain's belief in the people had more than a theoretical interest for him. In the aftermath of the capitulation of the Vichy regime to Nazi Germany, Maritain, involuntarily exiled in America, and Yves R. Simon, living in America, debated in correspondence and otherwise the proper course for France after the expected defeat of Germany. The debate centered on the political ambitions of General Charles de Gaulle and his relationship to the French freedom fighters.

Simon cast much of the blame for France's problems on the anti-democratic tradition of Thomism, de Gaulle being another authoritarian leader was welcomed by prominent Catholics. Maritain "placed his confidence . . . not in a man, it is in the people of our country that we have our best hope."[50]

Personalist democracy is a society dominated by man's spiritual nature in all of its goodness. The values of personalist society are formed by its culture, which is the "word of the spirit."[51] Maritain was clear that he considered a civilization worthy of that name *only* if it is a culture in which the spiritual dominates "taking the word *spiritual* [Maritain's emphasis] in its widest acceptation."[52] The true natural man, according to Maritain, is not Rousseau's noble savage, but the man of virtue imbued with moral and spiritual values that alone designate a true personality. In Maritain's scheme the dominant values of a body politic would be inculcated in the society by an educational system that included participation in the spiritual "transactions" noted above combined with a formal educational system that stressed the spiritual and moral tradition of the body politic. It is through this educational process that the "body politic" communicates the values that undergird the practical tenets of the moral charter that is the feature of the midlevel personalist democracy.

The end of the formal educational system is to produce persons, not individuals. Maritain remarked that "what is of most importance in educators themselves is a respect for the soul as well as for the body of the child, the sense of his innermost essence and his internal resources, and a sort of sacred and loving attention to his mysterious identity, which is a hidden thing that no techniques can reach."[53] The primary aim of education is "to guide man in the evolving dynamism through which he shapes himself as a human person—armed with knowledge, strength of judgment, and moral virtues . . . conveying to him the spiritual heritage of the nation and civilization. . . ."[54] The secondary aim is to shape man to lead a normal, useful and cooperative life in the community . . . awakening and strengthening both his sense of freedom and his sense of obligation and responsibility."[55]

When Maritain, therefore, advocates that the people concur in the moral charter by helping in the formation of moral attitudes he was presupposing an educational system that would inculcate spiritual values in the masses. Of course, Maritain saw those values as also being profoundly shaped by Christianity.

UNIVERSAL SUFFRAGE

Maritain's belief in the people was not just a theoretical construct. He believed in self-determination as actualized by freely choosing the type of government and the leaders of that government—the right to vote.[56] The right to vote, like all of the rights that inhere in citizens of Maritain's personalist democracy, is grounded in his concept of the person:

> A state of civilization in which men as individual persons, by a free choice designate those who shall hold authority, is in itself a more perfect state. For it is true that political authority has as its essential function the direction of free men towards the common good, it is normal for these free men to choose by themselves those who have the function of leading them: this is the most elementary form of active participation in political life. That is why universal suffrage, by means of which every adult human person has, as such, the right to make his opinion felt regarding the affairs of the community by casting his vote in the election of the people's representatives and officers of the State—that is why universal suffrage has a wholly fundamental political and human value and is one of those rights which a community of free men can never give up.[57]

Universal suffrage to Maritain meant that every adult citizen, male and female, young and old, "of whatever race and social condition" has the right to vote.[58] His repeated emphasis on every adult having the right to vote, without qualification, warrants the implication that only those convicted of serious crimes, children, and the mentally ill, do not have the right. The felon has lost this fundamental right by his antisocial conduct. The mentally ill have the right, but lack the capacity to exercise it. Children have the right since it is fundamental, but in the child the right is inchoate, ripening into a complete right when the child reaches its majority.

Maritain was aware that there is a risk in universal suffrage. "We know, indeed, that evil and foolishness are more frequent among men than intelligence and virtue." This is not a valid reason for limiting suffrage to the intelligent and cultivated for "experience shows that in politics . . . persons of education and refinement are no less often mistaken than the ignorant; the errors of the latter are vulgar, those of the former intellectualized and documented."[59] The central virtue for political leaders is prudence, which is "rare and difficult to acquire." In evaluating a potential leader's prudence, Maritain thought that intuition and instinct were better guides than intelligence and refinement.[60] In the selection of political leaders, Maritain followed his admonition noted above—trust the people.

The right to vote is part of the more general right of self-determination. Just as each person controls his own spiritual destiny by freely choosing whether to live a moral life, so also, each person has the innate right to choose the political leaders who can provide the environment for the spiritual life. For Maritain this right is basic to a democracy, a right that Christianity enhanced by its teaching of the right of all to choose or reject the moral life and the Christian teaching of the inherent equality of all before God. Voting is the exercise of the right to choose. Maritain's espousal of universal suffrage had implications beyond its importance in the selection of political leaders. A voter is also a citizen. By advocating universal suffrage Maritain was, at the same time, expanding the right of citizenship.

Adler and Farrell recognized that one of the critical differences between a democracy and a republic is that historically the latter have restricted citizenship:

> The Republic enslaves or subjects men who can and should be citizens. . . . even with the abolition of slavery . . . human beings may be excluded from suffrage for one of the following reasons: because they are females, . . . foreigners for whom naturalization is not made available; [others] because they lack sufficient property; because they are illiterate . . .; because of color, creed, or previous condition of servitude."[61]

In Maritain's democracy none of the above are impediments to citizenship. All adults can vote and are citizens. Adler and Farrell argued that democracy's moral superiority to the republican form of government lies partly in universal suffrage. Maritain would agree. But, he would add that universal suffrage and universal citizenship are in a large measure the result of the social gospel of Christianity.

John Stuart Mill, like Maritain, advocated universal suffrage, but Mill's reasons for doing so differed from Maritain's.[62] Universal suffrage for Mill was part of his belief in the citizen's right to active participation in government, a belief grounded on utility, not in the belief that universal suffrage is a right, even a right mandated by positive law. Voting cannot be a right for Mill because it is a "power over others."[63] Mill's position on voting vis-à-vis Maritain's is instructive. Universal suffrage for Mill is strictly utilitarian. For Maritain, universal suffrage is part of self-determination, an expression of the free will of the person, a part of self-determination tied to the spiritual nature of human beings. Mill's democracy is an instrument of his utilitarianism. Maritain's democracy is also instrumental, but it is an instrument to vivify man's higher nature, providing a peaceful environment for that nature to grow and prosper.

It is Mill not Maritain who has been followed by the western democracies. In the United States, for example, the right to vote is a precept of positive law that can be regulated or even abrogated by the state, as utilitarian considerations warrant. According to the United States Supreme Court, the right to vote is not a constitutionally protected right.[64] The Court has, however, restricted the states' right to regulate or interfere in the voting process.[65]

NOTES

1. Jacques Maritain, *Scholasticism and Politics* (New York: Macmillan Company, 1941), 94-95.

2. Ibid.,79.

3. Jacques Maritain, *Integral Humanism* (New York: Charles Scribner's Sons, 1968), 6.

4. Jacques Maritain, *Man and the State* (Chicago: The University of Chicago Press, 1951), 110.

5. Ibid., 110-111.

6. Ibid., 112-113.

7. Ibid.

8. See, *inter alia, Integral Humanism*, 42 and 218-219.

9. *Integral Humanism*, 10-11.

10. Jacques Maritain, *On The Philosophy of History*, ed. Joseph W. Evans (Clifton, New Jersey: Augustus M. Kelley, 1973), 9.

11. See Claes Ryn, "Historicism and its Critics," *Modern Age*, Summer/Fall, 1987, 343. The term "value-centered historicism" is Ryn's. Value-centered historicism is the view that "universality when it does reveal itself, does so only in historical, experiential particulars." Claes Ryn, "Universality and History: The Concrete as Normative," *Humanitas*, vol. VI, no. 1 (Fall, 1992/Winter, 1993): 10, 28. Value-centered historicism does not lapse into moral relativism.

Universal standards are not rejected. Ryn explains that "From the point of normative authority, concrete experience is primary, ideas secondary. It is certainly possible to speak of the good for man in ideas, but the meaning of the ideas must be ascertained in ideas and experience together. Theoretical accounts of universal value that cannot in some way appeal to concrete reality will remain unconvincing." Ibid., 32.

12. *Integral Humanism*, 138-139.

13. Ibid.

14. Ibid., 10.

15. *Range of Reason*, 168.

16. *Man and the State*, 114.

17. Ibid.

18. Ibid., 115.

19. Ibid.

20. *The Federalist* (No. 10, J. Madison) ed. Jacob E. Cooke (Middletown, Connecticut: Wesleyan University Press, 1961).

21. Ibid.

22. *Man and the State*, 119.

23. *Range of Reason*, 168.

24. *Man and the State*, 115.

25. Ibid., 116.

26. Ibid.

27. Ibid.

28. *Schenck v. U.S.*, 249 U.S. 47 (1919). Schenck and six coconsirators were charged with "causing and attempting to cause insubordination, etc., in the military and naval forces of the United States, and to obstruct the recruiting and enlistment service of the United States" by distributing and circulating to potential military recruits a seditious leaflet that "intimated that conscription was despotism in its worst form. . . ." Ibid.

29. Thomas I. Emerson, *The System of Freedom of Expression* (New York: Random House, 1970), 17, the classic exposition of the "clear and present danger" test.

30. *Man and the State*, 118.

31. Jacques Maritain, *The Responsibility of the Artist* (New York:, n.p., 1960), 79-80.

32. Ibid.

33. Ibid.

34. Ibid., 118-119.

35. John Courtney Murray, S.J., "Should There Be a Law?" *We Hold These Truths* (Kansas City, Missouri: Sheed and Ward, 1988), 155, 159.

36. Ibid., 162.

37. Ibid., 163.

38. Ibid., 170.

39. Ibid., 172.

40. Ibid.

41. Ibid., 173.

42. *Christianity and Democracy*, 59.

43. *Politics*, bk. III, ch. xv.

44. *Christianity and Democracy*, 60.

45. Jonathan Elliot, *The Debates in the Several State Conventions on the Adoption of the Federal Constitution as Recommended by the General Convention at Philadelphia in 1787*, Second Edition, 5 vols. (Philadelphia: J. B. Lippincott, 1986), II, 246. See also Cecelia M. Kenyon, *The Antifederalists*, foreword Gordon S. Wood (Boston: Northeastern University Press, 1985).

46. *Man and the State*, 143.

47. *Range of Reason*, 122.

48. Ibid.

49. *Politics*, bk. IV, ch. 4. Hippocrates G. Apostle disagrees with the classical translation of *demokratia* as the many, primarily the poor. Apostle says that a more correct translation of the word is "common people." He asks "Should *demokratia* be translated as 'democracy'?" He concludes that the best translation of *demokratia* is "common people's rule, for the common people as defined by Aristotle and as usually understood today are regarded as opposed to the upper classes." Aristotle, *Politics*, trans. and commentaries by Hippocrates G. Apostle and Lloyd P. Gerson (Grinnell, Iowa: The Peripatetic Press, 1986), 12-14. Apostle's translation of *demokratia* makes Maritain's definition of the "people" consistent with that of Aristotle.

50. John Hellman, "The Anti-Democratic Impulse in Catholicism: Jacques Maritain, Yves R. Simon, and Charles de Gaulle During World War II," *Journal of Church and State*, Vol. 33, Summer, 1991, 453, 456. Hellman's article is an excellent account of this troubling time for Maritain, Simon, and the French patriots.

51. *Religion and Culture*, 4.

52. Ibid.

53. See Jacques Maritain, *Education at the Crossroads* (New Haven: Yale University Press, 1943) 9.

54. Ibid., 10.

55. Ibid., 14-15.

56. Ibid., 47; *Man and the State*, 25-26; *Integral Humanism*, 175, n.

11; *Christianity and Democracy*, 59; *Scholasticism and Politics*, 112-113.

57. *The Rights of Man*, 47.

58. *Christianity and Democracy*, 59.

59. *Scholasticism and Politics*, 112.

60. Ibid., 113.

61. *The Thomist* VI, no. 2, 396.

62. John Stuart Mill, *Considerations on Representative Government* (London: Longman, Green, Longman, Roberts and Green, 1865) ch. III, 164-168.

63. Ibid., ch. x, 198-201. See also Dennis F. Thompson, *John Stuart Mill and Representative Government* (Princeton: Princeton University Press, 1976), 96.

64. *Rodriguez v. Popular Democratic Party*, 457 U.S. 1 (1982).

65. See *Anderson v. Celebrezze*, 460 U.S. 780 (1983); *Munro v. Socialist Workers Party*, 479 U.S. 189 (1986).

CHAPTER 5

CHRISTIANITY AND DEMOCRACY

Maritain believed that the Christianity-democracy relationship was symbiotic in that both are dependent upon and receive benefits from each other. This chapter will discuss the specifics of that symbiosis. Elements of the symbiosis have been previously analyzed as part of Maritain's political ontology that was grounded in his existentialist Thomism, in his concept of the moral charter, and in his concept of spirituality as a necessary force in a democratic political order. The red thread running through the fabric of the earlier discussion was Maritain's blending of Christianity, through his interpretation of being and the person, with democracy. In this chapter the blending process continues as the discussion turns to Maritain's political theology and then to the practical elements of the Christianity-democracy symbiosis.

THE PERSON AND CHRISTIANITY

The idea of the person was not indigenous to Christianity. In the Old Testament the word "heart" was used to designate the spiritual nature.[1] Jeremiah and the other prophets called for a spiritual response, "from within," beyond external appearances, "And you, O desolate one, what do you mean that you dress in scarlet, that you deck yourself with ornaments of gold, that you enlarge your eyes with paint: in vain you beautify yourself."[2] The Greeks also developed the concept of the soul. Clark points out that Homer's "eschatological *psyche*" designated the soul in contrast to *soma*, which was used to designate "the living body instead of the corpse. . . . The Pythagorean teaching of the significance of number as a principle of knowledge, of cosmic order, and of harmony in human life (public and private) relates to an intellectual and moral aspect of the human soul, today called self-transcendence."[3] Plato, Aristotle, and Plotinus wrote about the transcendental nature of man.[4] Stoicism and Neo-Platonism also stressed the importance of man's spiritual nature.[5]

The Greeks, nevertheless, did not attain a "metaphysic of personality," although they had the analytical skills and the metaphysical principles to do so. Aristotle, for example, because he "did not share the Christian solicitude to base the unity of the individual on the spirit" failed to grasp the full significance of personality.[6] The Christian philosophy of the Mediaeval Age took the foundation laid by the Greeks, combined it with the gospel, to add flesh to the bones of the person as a philosophical concept:

> And finally, to return once more to our starting-point and basic principle, how could personality be anything but the mark of being at the very summit of its perfection, in a philosophy like the Christian philosophy where everything is suspended from the creative act of a personal God? For all things were made by the Word, and the Word is with God, and the Word is God; that is to say precisely this being Who presents Himself as personal in virtue of the fact that He presents Himself as Being. Christian personalism also like the rest, has its root in the metaphysic of Exodus; we are persons because we are the work of a Person; we participate in His personality even as, being good, we participate in His perfection; being causes, in His creative power; being prudent in His Providence; and, in a word, as beings in His being.[7]

According to Maritain, the idea of the person was fully developed in the Christian doctrines of the Trinity and the Incarnation:

> It is in a theological form and at the peak of the most abstract conceptualization, that the notions of person and personality were first explicitly offered to the human mind: namely, in the dogmatic formulas concerned with Christian faith in the divine Trinity—one Nature in three Persons—and in the Incarnation of the Word—a divine Person assuming human nature. At the same time the human mind was confronted with a new idea of man—the Gospels and St. Paul disclosed to it the prevalence of the internal man over the external man, of the inner life of the soul over legal or exterior forms—and it could contemplate in the Son of Man crowned with thorns the abysmal depth of the most living and mysterious self.[8]

The word "Person" when used in connection with the Trinity designates the fullness of the spiritual nature of the Divine Being. The doctrine of the Trinity emphasizes the spiritual bond that subsists in the one God composed of three persons. The unity of the Trinity is reflected in the spiritual bond that exists between persons in the political order, a unity that leads to the formation of the political community. The three Persons of the Trinity are all equal, reflecting for Maritain the inherent spiritual equality of each human person; all are endowed with a spiritual nature; all are equal before God. The doctrine of the Trinity also emphasizes love, love of the Father for the Son. The Holy Spirit symbolizes that love. The Incarnation is the manifestation of the spiritual in the temporal world. God became man, but retained His divinity, His spirituality in matter, the physical body of Jesus Christ. From the divine love of the Father for the Son flows the love of the Father for all of his creatures. And from this love flows the Christian doctrine of love of neighbor which grounds Maritain's conception of a democracy imbued with friendship and concord.

Maritain saw a relationship between the person and the Absolute because it is only in the latter that the person can be completely fulfilled. The person's "spiritual fatherland is the whole order of goods, having an absolute value, and which serve as an introduction to the absolute Whole which transcends the world."[9] In other words, the person's spirituality is reflective of a higher, transcendent spirituality that embodies the absolute of the Good, the True, the Beautiful, and Being as Being, all united in God. Finally, according to Maritain, the person resembles God in a "proper and peculiar fashion. It is the image of God. For God is spirit, and the person proceeds from Him, having as a principle of life, a spiritual soul, a spirit capable of knowing and loving."[10] Through divine grace the person can "participate in the very life of God, so as to finally love Him and know Him even as He knows and loves himself."[11]

Maritain is alluding to the proposition that it is the spiritual nature of man that, through contemplation, can know God. The Christian mystic Walter Hilton expressed the same thought, "But it [the soul] recognizes Him as a changeless Being, as sovereign Power, sovereign Truth, and sovereign Goodness, and as the source of blessing, life, and eternal bliss."[12] This is the absolute good that Dostoevsky was referring to in *Notes from Underground* and the plenary good that was part of Bergson's spiritual intuition in *The Two Sources of Morality and Religion*. Individuality, matter, is foreclosed by its very nature from knowledge or love of God. Nor can individuality ever approach the absolute values of the Good, the True, and the Beautiful because matter does not have the potentiality to become spiritual.

ART AND THE PERSON

Maritain illustrated the theological origins of the person by tracing the depiction of the person's spiritual nature in art. He identified a "first phase" in which the:

> mystery of the Person comes into sight as a mere object in the world of Things but transcending Things. Here we have Byzantine art—so close in one sense, to Oriental art, though freer from Things—with its glorious and royal, not suffering Christs. . . . The immense reality of the human soul is more and more present, but not revealed, even in the manner of an object. . . . The divinity of Christ soars over everything.[13]

In the second phase, the age of Gothic art, while the person is still an object in the world of things, "Art is still dominated by sacred inspiration, and Christ is still at the center. But this time it is Christ in His humanity, in His torment and redeeming passion. . . . The human soul gleams everywhere through the barred windows of the objective world. . . ."[14] In the third phase, "the sense of the human Self and of human subjectivity enters a process of internalization. . . ." exemplified in the "Renaissance, baroque art, and our classical art." In this phase although the external object was given preference, still "painters did not strive for external resemblance. The external form was not to be copied, but to be interpreted."[15] In this phase, the religious symbols of Christianity were used to illustrate the substratum of spirituality that exists behind the external facade of the individual.

Finally, there is the art of the modern era. In this phase Western art has:

> plunged more and more into the individual, incommunicable universe of created subjectivity. . . . [art has also] been busy revealing and expressing the secret aspects and infinitely varied meanings of Things, whose visibility conceals but can, by virtue of man's spiritual power, reveal the ocean of being. . . .
>
> On the other hand, when art primarily intent on the artist's Self succeeds in revealing creative subjectivity, it does also reveal obscurely Things and their hidden aspects and meanings—and with greater power of penetration indeed, I mean into the depths of Corporeal Being itself and this Nature that our hands touch . . . the poetic perception which animates art catches and manifests at the same time what matters most in Things, the transapparent reality and secret

significance on which they live.[16]

In the first and second phases, the Christian religion's symbols were a gateway to man's inner nature. Christianity was the guiding light of the early artistic efforts by expressly recognizing this spiritual nature. In the last two phases Christianity had established through its teaching the primacy of the soul as the source of man's dignity and spirituality so that even though art focuses on the self, it is the spiritual aspect of the self that the artist is trying to capture. The idea of the person developed first theologically, then through art, until finally the concept was brought into the political order.

The theological creation of the person was the work of Christianity, not just Catholicism. Martin Luther's comments on man's dual nature are representative of Protestant thought:

> Man has a twofold nature, a spiritual and a bodily one. According to the spiritual nature, which men refer to as the soul, he is called a spiritual, inner, or new man. According to the bodily nature, which men refer to as the flesh, he is called a carnal, outward, or old man of whom the Apostle writes in II Cor. 4 [:16], "Through our outer nature is wasting away, our inner nature is being renewed every day."[17]

The person then developed from its adumbration in Greek philosophy into a uniquely Christian theological concept, which was eventually carried over from theology to political philosophy. During its developmental period, by emphasizing the inherent dignity of each human being, a dignity that was in opposition to the unity of a political order imposed from above, and the right of the human person to control his own destiny in the private sphere of morality and the public sphere of politics, the Christian concept of the person gave impetus to the spirit of freedom and equality that other historical forces had set in motion; historical forces that Tocqueville noted were moving ineluctably toward democracy.

Maritain more than any other political theorist applied the Christian concept of man's spiritual nature to politics in general and democracy in particular. The person's importance to Maritain's personalist and Christian-inspired democracies has been discussed above. The person is also at the root of the neo-Thomist doctrine of the origin of political authority, which was given an expansive reinterpretation by Maritain and Yves R. Simon. Their reinterpretation forged another link in the chain uniting Christianity and democracy.

THE PERSON AND POLITICAL AUTHORITY

This part of the discussion begins with a threshold question: What is the source of political authority? Maritain's answer was that all authority "derives from God as from its primordial source."[18] God must be the source of all authority because Christianity teaches that all men are equal in the eyes of their creator. Since the person is primarily a spiritual being who shares in the spirituality of the Absolute, "we grasp in the moral order that no man possesses authority over another, except as this authority derives from the sovereignty of the Cause of being . . . has in God the immediate ground of its moral value."[19]

Since all authority came from God, Maritain said that "no particular group of men has the right to rule others."[20] Even those who are best qualified to rule, the virtuous, have no inherent right to do so. Here, Maritain partially rejected Aristotle's claim that the "superior in virtue ought to rule, or be master."[21] The virtuous few, or the one who is most virtuous, may rule, according to Maritain, but only after being chosen to do so by the many. Nothing, neither noble birth, wealth, or even virtue, gives anyone an inherent right to rule. The break with Aristotle is partial because Maritain did not reject the proposition that the virtuous *should* rule, only that the virtuous *ought to* rule in the sense that the virtuous have an inherent right to do so.

Political authority flows from God not to political leaders directly, but through the people then to political leaders:

> from the creative and conservative principle of nature through the channels of nature itself, that is, through the consent or the will of the people, or of the body of the community, through which authority always passes before being invested in the leaders. . . . Once the man of common humanity has understood that he is born with the right to conduct his own life by himself, as a being responsible for his acts before God . . ., how can the people be expected to obey those who govern unless it is because the latter have received from the people themselves the custody of the people's common good.[22]

The idea that the people are the conduit for political authority from God to political leaders is not original with Maritain. The issue of the origin of political authority had been analyzed by neo-Thomist political theorists, William of Ockham, Marsilius of Padua, and Francisco Suarez in the context of the battle between the Pope and the civil rulers in the Mediaeval period. Ockham and Marsilius found no scriptural evidence that the Holy Roman Emperor received his political authority directly from God. Instead, Ockham held that the people are the repository of all political authority by virtue of being created equal by God. They transfer their authority to the political leader.[23] Although Ockham, Marsilius, and Suarez did not use the term "person" in their analysis, the person is the ultimate ground for their conclusions.

Marsilius also found ultimate political authority in the people. His definition of law included public opinion as reflecting the consent of the community about the right course of conduct for the body politic.[24] The practical side of law as public opinion embodies the power to enforce the people's wishes, a *praeceptum coactivum*, or coercive sanction, "a principle of right supported by the force necessary to put it into execution."[25] The source of law is the whole body of citizens:

> We declare that according to the Truth and to the opinion of Aristotle, the Lawgiver, that is the primary, essential and efficient source of law is the People, that is the whole body of citizens or a majority of them, acting of their own free choice openly declared in a general assembly of the citizens and proscribing something to be done or not done in regard to civil affairs under penalty of temporal punishment. I say a majority taking into account of the whole number of persons in the community over which the law is to be exercised. It makes no difference whether the whole body of citizens or its majority acts of itself immediately or whether it entrusts the matter to one or more persons to act for it.[26]

Emerton understood the word *veritas* as used by Marsilius in the quotation above "and in many other passages [of *The Defensor Pacis*] as synonymous with the Gospel."[27] Gospel passages that proclaim the people's freedom include: "For freedom Christ has set us free; stand fast therefore, and do not submit again to a yoke of slavery;[28] and "The Lord is spirit, and where the Spirit of the Lord is, there is freedom."[29] Emerton believed, and a close reading of Marsilius supports the belief, that Marsilius was referring to these or similar biblical passages to show that the people's freedom included the power to choose their political leaders, a power that the people derived from God. Marsilius deviated from the conventional wisdom of mediaeval scholastics that once the people transferred authority they could not take it back even if the transferee, most often a king, abused his power. Marsilius left a residual right in the people to terminate the transfer and divest the transferee at any time he did not govern for the common good. Exactly what type of conduct by a king would warrant the abrogation of the grant of authority by the people was not discussed.

The importance of Ockham and Marsilius for Maritain's political theory cannot be underestimated. Ockham's nominalism has been extensively criticized for its alleged destructiveness of classical mediaeval and Thomistic philosophy. The whole thrust of nominalism and the controversy over the Pope's temporal power should be viewed as part of the irresistible move toward democracy noted by Tocqueville. Thus, Ockham and Marsilius are important steps in the process of the Christian and Catholic part of that movement that culminated in Maritain, a movement that reconciled democracy with Christianity and a movement that eventually evolved into a political theory that viewed democracy as the best instrument to implement the Christian social gospel.[30]

Ockham's and Marsilius's claim of the plenary power of the people with its concomitant principle that there is no special individual or group that is inherently entitled to rule, not even those who allegedly are the most virtuous, was developed by Maritain into a political philosophy of democracy—after Ockham's and Marsilius's principle had been amplified by the Spanish neo-Thomist Francisco Suarez. This is not to claim that Maritain embraced Ockham's nominialism. Maritain did not.[31]

Simon used Suarez's rationale to posit what might be termed a divine right of democracy. While Maritain did not expressly subscribe to Simon's interpretation of Suarez, a close reading of Maritain leads little doubt that he supported Simon's exegesis. Indeed given the relationship of the two thinkers it is possible that Maritain was the inspiration for Simon's analysis.

Simon started with Maritain's idea that the person, the spiritual being who unites with other persons to form the root of Maritain's political order, has an inherent right to rule himself based on his spiritual nature that comes from God. The authority to rule also comes from God who is the creator of all things. Simon cited Suarez:

> Primarily, the supreme civil power, considered in itself, is given immediately by God to men assembled into a city or perfect political community; this does not take place by a peculiar and, as it were, positive disposition or by a donation entirely distinct from the production of such nature; it takes place by way of natural consequences from the first creation of such a nature: therefore, as a result of such donation this [supreme civil power] is not placed in one person or in any peculiar group but in the whole complete people, or in the body of the community.[32]

Suarez claimed that political power "resides only in the community, inasmuch as it is necessary to the preservation of the latter and inasmuch

as it can be manifested by the judgment of the natural reason."[33] If God
had placed political power in one person, a "special grant" would have
been necessary and "there would be need that [the special grant] be
manifested to men through revelation, so that they [men] might be sure
about it. . . ."[34] Revelation, of course, does not speak of such a direct
disposition. Suarez continued:

> But all the natural reason shows is that this power is necessary to the
> community as a whole; it does not show that this is necessary in one
> person or in a senate; therefore, in so far as it is from God immediately,
> it is merely understood to be in the community as a whole, not in any
> particular part of it. . . . The natural reason cannot conceive of *any
> cause by which political power would be immediately placed in one
> person . . . or group of persons* [my emphasis] within the community,
> rather than in another person or group of persons; therefore, in so far as
> it is procured by nature, political power does not reside immediately in
> any subject except in the community itself.[35]

Simon concluded that the natural reason "does not decide, either, that
the political regime should be monarchy or aristocracy." Simon asked,
"But then does it not follow that democracy is of immediate divine
institution?" Simon said that the proposition should be denied if "by
'institution' is meant a disposition of a *positive* [Simon's emphasis]
character." But, if democracy is a natural institution, then, Simon said that
the proposition must be accepted. Monarchy and aristocracy cannot be
established except by a positive disposition. That is a person or specific
group of persons, i.e., the virtuous, must be designated.[36]
Democracy, however, needs no positive designation since political
power is naturally in the community, the many. Political power naturally
resides in the community because according to the Christian religion, man
has the capacity to rule himself. Suarez explained:

> man was made after the image of God alone, and therefore it does not
> seem justly possible to reduce him into the service of, or subjection to
> any man; therefore one man cannot be compelled to recognize another
> as a prince and temporal lord; and therefore a political principate which
> usurps this dominion is neither lawful nor from God.[37]

The natural power to rule is manifested first in the moral order. Man
has the freedom to chose between good or evil. This freedom to choose is
manifested in the political order, which for Maritain—and Simon—was a
part of the moral or ethical order. Political power, then, flows from God to

the many who are the community in its formative stage. The many, according to Suarez, and Maritain and Simon concur, can elect to establish a monarchy, aristocracy, oligarchy, or democracy. Whatever formal type of government is created by the many, if that form provides for legal equality and ultimate power in the many, it is a democracy, according to Maritain, because it is animated by democratic principles.

In *Scholasticism and Politics*, written ten years before *Philosophy of Democratic Government*, Maritain, with Suarez as his source, stated that in a democracy, rulers "hold their authority only from the designation of the people." He continued that what is true of democracy is also true "for all regimes, whatever they are"—their authority derives from their subjects. All authority proceeds directly from being and ultimately from the "transcendent source" of being, God.[38] Authority proceeds from being in the sense that authority appeals to conscience, to the moral or spiritual part of being. The ultimate source of all being and all authority is Being, God.

In *Scholasticism and Politics*, "in order to avoid all ambiguities," Maritain commented on Abraham's Lincoln's "famous address of 1863" where "of the people, by the people, for the people" was used.[39] The phrase meant, Maritain stated, that "a government exercised in the virtue of the people's mission, in the virtue of the popular designation of authority, which passes authority over to its holders, according to the duration, the measure, and the degree of their attributions."[40] Maritain's comment is a paraphrase of Suarez.

The United States Constitution reflects Suarez's and ultimately what became Maritain's rationale, a rationale that was also central to the Federalist Party's constitutional theory. Chief Justice John Marshall, an ardent Federalist, was clear in one of the early seminal cases in the Constitutional history of the United States, *M'Culloch v. Maryland, et al.*, that the American democracy rested on the people as the fount of political authority. Marshall said that the people "were at perfect liberty" to accept or reject the proposed Constitution. The fact that the people acted in state ratification conventions did not mean that the individual states were the depository of ultimate sovereignty. The convention system was only used as a convenience for the expression of the people's will.

Marshall also accepted the people's right to divest or modify the government formed under the Articles of Confederation even though it had been the states that had legitimately formed the Confederation. According to Marshall, "the government of the Union then (whatever may be the influence of this fact on the case), is emphatically, and truly, a government of the people. In form and in substance it emanates from them. Its powers are granted by them, and are to be exercised directly on them, and for their benefit."[41]

In *Man and the State*, Maritain again relied on Suarez. Maritain rejected the contention that the people are only an instrument through which authority is transmitted to establish a monarchy, aristocracy, oligarchy, or democracy, as the people choose. Whatever formal type of government is created by the many, if that form provides for legal equality and ultimate power in the many, it is a democracy according to Maritain because it is animated by democratic principles. The people have an inherent right to self-government. The people possess political power directly from God. Even after the people "invest certain men" with political power, the people nevertheless keep their right to self-government and the concomitant authority to rule themselves. The ruler is merely the agent of the people. As such the ruler's authority is derivative and secondary to the people's inherent right. For good cause the people can divest the ruler of his derivative authority at any time.[42] Although he never expressly stated his belief in the divine institution of democracy, a close reading of Maritain's texts cited above, combined with the writings of Simon, leave little doubt that Maritain believed in democracy's divine origin, which from the foregoing is directly related to the Christian religion.

Maritain's position as derived from Suarez is opposed to the social contract theories of Thomas Hobbes, Rousseau, and John Locke. Maritain's disagreements with Rousseau have been sufficiently explored above so as not to warrant additional comment here. Hobbes was clear that once the commonwealth was formed by the individual promises of the members of the community, the individual members become "subjects," who cannot thereafter change the form of government.[43] If the subjects attempt to change the form of government and some are killed in the process, Hobbes said that the dead "are the author[s] of [their] own punishment." The depraved nature of man was, for Hobbes, the progenitor of political society. Rather than a spiritual bond, Hobbes's political order is held together by force, for covenants "without the sword, are but words, and of no strength to secure a man at all."[44] Once Christian concepts such as the person with its theological origins and the divine institution of democracy are accepted, the foundation is laid for a political order that respects and fosters the spiritual nature of man and rejects force as a basis for political order.

Hobbes's political theory stands in sharp contrast to Maritain's Christian-infused democracy. For Maritain, the formation of the body politic was not forced on the individuals in prepolitical society by fear of their fellow human beings. Nor was the body politic made necessary by the requirement for an impartial arbitrator of disputes between citizens, as

Locke claimed. The body politic flowed from the acts of being as an inevitable consequence of manifestations of those acts. Suarez said and Maritain agreed that:

> it can be argued, as I was above saying, granted the will of men to come together in a political community, it is not in their power to impede this jurisdiction; therefore the indication proximately is not to come forth from the wills of them as from a proper efficient cause. Just as in matrimony we rightly gather that the husband is the head of the wife from the grant of the Author of nature himself, not from the will of the wife, because, though they by their wills draw together in matrimony, yet if they contract matrimony they cannot impede this superiority.[45]

The beings/persons who make up the body politic always retain the ultimate authority and as Marshall indicated in *M'Culloch v. Maryland*, can, at any time, change the form of their government. In *Man and the State*, Maritain was critical of Hobbes's Leviathan or "Mortal God" as Maritain termed the Hobbesian absolute ruler. Maritain was clear that it is the people who are sovereign, not Hobbes's absolute ruler, be that ruler one man or many.[46]

What is most noteworthy about the foregoing discussion is that the warrant for the people's plenary power, as actualized in the democratic principle, is Christianity. For Maritain there is no kind of autocracy, however benign, that can actualize the democratic principle because such a regime will not subject itself to the plenary power of the people. As alluded to earlier, even a republican type of government that does not provide for universal suffrage is deficient in the democratic principle.

The republic is a less just regime than the personalist democracy and the Christian-inspired democracy. The same for an oligarchy. Each of the defective regimes denies Christianity's contribution, more or less, to the democratic principle by not recognizing the inherent equality, spirituality, and liberty of all persons. When Christianity's part in the equation is removed, the democratic principle disintegrates. Without Christianity's warrant, according to Maritain, democracy lacks a true philosophical base. Being as spirituality is subverted.

Maritain would concede that the recognition of man's spiritual nature with all that it entails is not endemic to Christianity. There have been religio-philosophical foundations of political order not based on Christianity, but on rational or humanistic conceptions of equality and freedom, which inevitably result in an anarchic or bourgeois liberal democracy that substitutes man as individual as the philosophical base of the regime. Maritain would respond that these attempts either lean so heavily on Christian principles, for example the inherent dignity of man, that in truth, Christianity, or the perversion of Christianity, is the warrant for the regime. The ultimate ground for human dignity is being. And the Christian concept of the person is grounded on Being as Being, as has been shown above. For Maritain, rationalistic attempts to ground being outside of its divine origins are simply perversions of the Christian concept.

Maritain did not believe that every Christian must be a democrat. "One can be a Christian and achieve one's salvation while militating in favor of any political regime whatsoever," provided that the political regime one favors does not violate natural law and God's commandments. The Christians who lived under the Roman Empire and accepted the institution of slavery did not forfeit their chance for eternal salvation, although the Roman Empire with its class distinctions was not imbued with the democratic principle. In the political order, democracy's link with Christianity is not forged because Christianity is a religious creed, but with Christianity as the "leaven in the social and political life of nations and a bearer of the temporal hope of mankind. . . . It is in the depths of the secular conscience and secular existence that Christianity works."[47] Maritain is convincing when he said that Christianity's influence is pervasive:

> It was not given to believers faithful to Catholic dogma, but to rationalists to proclaim in France the rights of man and of the citizen, to Puritans to strike the last blow at slavery in America, to atheistic communists to abolish in Russia the absolutism of private profit. This last process would have been less vitiated by the force of error and would have occasioned fewer catastrophes, had it been performed by Christians. Yet the effort to deliver labor and man from the domination of money is an outgrowth of the currents released in the world by the preaching of the Gospel, such as the effort to abolish servitude and the effort to bring about the rights of the human person.[48]

The foregoing has focused on the theoretical foundation of Maritain's linking of Christianity and democracy. The next chapter will empirically test Maritain's claim by comparing Maritain's theory of democracy with Tocqueville's observations of the American democracy.

NOTES

1. Hans Walter Wolff, *Anthropology of the Old Testament* (Philadelphia: Fortress Press, 1974) as cited in Mary T. Clark, "An Inquiry into Personhood," *The Review of Metaphysics*, vol. XLVI, No. 1, (September, 1992): 3. I am indebted to Clark's article for the citations and other material tracing the history of the concept of the person. She does not mention Maritain.

2. "An Inquiry into Personhood" citing 4; Jeremiah 4:30, from Timothy Polk, *The Prophetic Persona: Jeremiah and the Language of the Self* (Sheffield: JSOT Press, 1984).

3. "An Inquiry into Personhood," 5.

4. Ibid. Clark mentions, *inter alia*, *Laches* 185e, *Laws* 896e-897b, *Nichomachean Ethics*, 78a-b, 1112a18-1113a16, 1100a10-1101a21. See also C. L. Griswold, *Self-Knowledge in Plato's Phaedrus* (New Haven: Yale University Press, 1986). For Plotinus, see *Enneads*, 4.3.27, 4.8.18, 4.7.1, 5.7.1., A. H. Armstrong, "Form, Individual, and Person in Plotinus," *Dionysius* 1 (1977): 49-69.

5. See Gerard Verbeke, *The Presence of Stoicism in Medieval Thought* (Washington, D.C.: Catholic University of America Press, 1983) and Edmund Colledge and Bernard McGinn, trans. and introduction, *Meister Eckhart*, The Classics of Western Spirituality Series (New York: Paulist Press, 1981).

6. Etienne Gilson, *The Spirit of Mediaeval Philosophy* (Notre Dame, Indiana: University of Notre Dame Press, 1991), 190, 200.

7. Ibid., 204-205.

8. Jacques Maritain, *Creative Intuition in Art and Poetry* (New York: Pantheon Books, 1953), 21.

9. *Scholasticism and Politics*, 64.

10. Ibid.

11. Ibid.

12. Walter Hilton, *The Ladder of Perfection*, trans. Leo Sherley-Price, intro. Clifton Wolters (New York: Penguin Books, 1988), ch. 32.

13. *Creative Intuition in Art and Poetry*, 22.

14. Ibid.

15. Ibid., 23.

16. Ibid., 33.

17. Martin Luther, *A Treatise on Christian Liberty*, trans. W. A. Lambert, ed. Harold J. Grimm (Philadelphia: Fortress Press, 1957), 7.

18. *Scholasticism and Politics*, 104.

19. Ibid., 105.

20. *Christianity and Democracy*, 41.

21. *Politics*, bk. I, ch. 6; bk. II, ch. 9; bk. III, ch. 4.

22. *Christianity and Democracy*, 41.

23. *A Short Discourse on Tyrannical Government*, bk. iv, chaps. 6, 8.

24. *Defender of the Peace*, bk. I as translated in Ephraim Emerton, *The Defensor Pacis of Marsiglio of Padua: A Critical Study*, Harvard Theological Series, VIII (Cambridge: Harvard University Press, 1920), 22-24.

25. Ibid., 24.

26. Ibid.

27. Ibid., n. 1.

28. 5 Gal. 1. (Christian Community).

29. 2 Cor. 3:17 (Christian Community).

30. A detailed discussion of the philosophical controversy surrounding Ockham far exceeds the scope of this study. For some Ockham's "early work in theology and philosophy shattered an admirable thesis of biblical faith and Greek reason achieved preeminently by Aquinas, in a proceeding golden age of scholasticism. In another view the same work is a "harvest, not a devastation of earlier Christian reflection." A. S. McGrade in his introduction to *A Short Discourse on Tyrannical Government*, xv. As far as political philosophy is concerned, this study views Ockham, Marsilius, Suarez, and Maritain as intellectual kinsmen.

Marsilius's political theory also has created controversy. Space limitations preclude a discussion of the controversy except as it affects Marsilius's relationship to Maritain's theory of democracy. In his "Marsilius of Padua" in Leo Strauss and Joseph Cropsey, ed. *History of Political Philosophy*, 3rd ed. (Chicago: University of Chicago Press, 1987), 273-295, Strauss in a somewhat denigrating critique of Marsilius emphasized what Strauss perceived as inconsistencies in the *Defender of the Peace*. Emerton said that the apparent inconsistency between Marsilius's "defense of democracy and at the same time the advocacy of the imperial rights," disappears when one follows carefully Marsiglio's analysis of the imperial office as the representation of the ultimate right of the people. *The Defensor Pacis of Marsiglio of Padua: A Critical Study*, 22.

See also Alan Gewirth, *Marsilius of Padua*, 2 vols. (New York: Columbia University Press, 1951). Gewirth's translation of *Defender of the Peace* differs from Emerton's. According to Gewirth, the passage quoted in footnote 27 should read that ultimate political authority is in the people "or the weightier part thereof." Marsilius explained that by "the weightier part thereof" he meant "to take into consideration the quantity and the quality of the persons in that community over which the law is made." *Defender of the Peace*, bk. I, ch. XII. Gerwith's translation does not impugn Emerton's translation or Marsilius's place as a nascent neo-Thomist democrat. For example, Gewirth noted that for Marsilius "the people's authority becomes absolutely unlimited." *Marsilius of Padua*, 311.

Gerwith also noted the differences in interpreting Marsilius. While some interpretations support this study's view of Marsilius as a democrat, other interpretations show a wide divergence to the point of interpreting Marsilius as an proponent of totalitarian government. Ibid., 304. Gerwith is adamant—"Marsilius is emphatically not totalitarian, for he insists that the unlimited authority can belong only to the whole people from which alone both the laws and the government must derive their authority." Ibid., 311. The better reasoned interpretation of Marsilius supports Gerwith and this study that Marsilius was a democrat.

31. See Jacques Maritain, *The Degrees of Knowledge*, trans. from the fourth French edition by Gerald B. Phelan (New York: Charles Scribner's Sons, 1959), esp. 93, 130.

32. Francisco Suarez, *De summa pontificus supra temorales reges excellentia, et potestate, Cap.* 2: "Utrum principatus politicus immediate a Deo sit, seu ex divina institutione," *Opera*, XXI (Venetiis, 1749) 114 ff. As cited in Yves R. Simon, *Philosophy of Democratic Government* (Chicago: University of Chicago Press, 1951), 172-173.

33. Ibid.

34. Francisco Suarez, *Defense of the Faith*, Bk. III, ch. II, trans. Geo. A. Moore, The Moore Series of Source Books (Chevy Chase, Maryland: Country Dollar Press, 1950).

35. *Philosophy of Democratic Government*, 172-173.

36. Ibid.

37. *Defense of the Faith*, bk. III, ch. I.

38. *Scholasticism and Politics*, 105-106.

39. Abraham Lincoln, "Gettysburg Address" [final draft] 19 November 1863, in *Abraham Lincoln's Speeches and Writings* (Birmingham. Alabama: Gryphon Editions, 1991), 2:536.

40. *Scholasticism and Politics*, 107.

41. 17 U.S. (4 Wheat) 316, 404 (1819).

42. *Man and the State*, 128-129.

43. Thomas Hobbes, *Leviathan*, The Second Part, ch. 18.

44. Ibid., ch. 17.

45. *Laws and God the Lawgiver*, chap. III.

46. *Man and the State*, 36-44.

47. *Christianity and Democracy*, 29.
48. Ibid., 30.

CHAPTER 6

RELIGION AND DEMOCRACY

Although Tocqueville described a democracy limited to a specific time and place, America in the 1830s, his comments were meant to apply to democracy generally:

> It is not then to satisfy a legitimate curiosity that I have examined America; my wish has been to find instruction by which we may ourselves profit. . . .; I have not even affected to discuss whether the social revolution, which I believe to be irresistible, is advantageous to mankind; I have acknowledged this revolution as a fact already accomplished or on the eve of its accomplishment; and I have selected the nation from amongst those which have undergone it, in which its development has been the most peaceful and the most complete, in order to discern its natural consequences, and, if possible, to distinguish the means by which it may be rendered profitable. I confess that in America I saw more than America; I sought the image of democracy itself, with its inclinations, its character, its prejudices, and its passions, in order to learn what we have to fear or to hope from its progress.[1]

In this section, the discussion will focus on certain tendencies inherent in all democracies, according to Tocqueville—atomization or unbridled individualism and materialism. It is these inherent tendencies that Tocqueville and Maritain believed must be tempered by Christianity for a democracy to have sustained viability as a form of government.

DEMOCRACY'S MORAL CHARTER

It was stated earlier that Maritain believed that democracy must have a moral charter. The importance that Maritain attached to this requirement can be seen in his scathing criticism of bourgeois liberal democracy, empty headed precisely because it had no moral charter. Maritain and

Tocqueville believed that Christianity could provide the moral charter.

The two thinkers start from the same basic premise, as stated by Tocqueville:

> Religion perceives that civil liberty affords a noble exercise to the faculties of man, and that a political world is prepared by the creator for the efforts of the intelligence. Contented with the freedom and the power which it enjoys in its own sphere, and with the place which it occupies, the empire of religion is never more surely established than when it reigns in the hearts of men unsupported by aught beside its native strength.
>
> Religion is no less the companion of liberty in all its battles and triumphs; the cradle of its infancy and the divine source of its claims. The safeguard of morality is religion, and morality is the best security of law, and the surest pledge of freedom.[2]

Religion, specifically Christianity for Maritain and Tocqueville, provided the moral charter that distinguishes for Maritain the personalist or Christian-inspired democracies from the Rousseauistic or bourgeois liberal, perverted democracies. Both thinkers recognized that law and institutions are incapable by themselves of providing a restraining force on the darker side of human nature, the side that expresses itself in unbridled human rapaciousness.

In a letter to his good friend Claude-François de Corcelle, Tocqueville was clear about this:

> You say that institutions are only half of my subject. I go farther than you, and I say that they are not even half. You know my ideas well enough that I accord institutions only a secondary influence on the destiny of men. Would to God I believed more in the omnipotence of institutions! I would have more hope for my future, because by chance we might someday stumble onto the precious piece of paper that would contain the recipe of all wrongs, or the man who knew the recipe. But alas there is no such thing, and I am quite convinced that political societies are not what their laws make them, but what sentiments, beliefs, ideas, habits of the heart, and the spirit of the men who form them, prepare them in advance to be, as well as what nature and education have made them.[3]

The "subject" that Tocqueville was referring to was *Democracy in America*. Earlier in the letter Tocqueville mentioned that he had reread a recent letter from Corcelle "and it seems to me that you were mistaken about the meaning of what I said when we were talking about my new book."[4] The second volume of *Democracy in America* appeared in 1840. The only other "new book" could have been Tocqueville's *Recollections*, which was written in 1850-51, but not published until 1893.[5] In 1846, he did write *Notice sur Cherbourg* a history of that city, but in that book political and social theory were not discussed.

In *Democracy in America*, Tocqueville had emphasized that it is society's sentiments and beliefs, in a word it is the culture of society, that determine what society will be. In his letter Tocqueville told Corcelle that "if this Truth" about the superiority of culture "does not emerge at every turn" from what was said in *Democracy in America*, then "I will not have attained the principal and, as it were, unique goal that I have in view."[6]

Christianity's restraining force is needed for a democracy more than any other type of government because in a democracy liberty is exalted so that the inherent weakness of laws, institutions, etc. to restrain is exacerbated. Tocqueville noted that in America, for example, "Thus whilist the law permits the Americans to do what they please, religion prevents them from conceiving and forbids them to commit what is rash or unjust."[7] This is the point that Bergson was getting at in *The Two Sources of Morality and Religion* and Dostoevsky in *Notes from Underground* and his other works.

Maritain and Tocqueville differed from Madison and the other framers of the American Constitution who put the primary emphasis on the institutions of government to restrain human passions by diffusing power among the three separate branches. Madison remarked that "Had every Athenian been a Socrates, every Athenian assembly would still have been a mob."[8] In *Federalist* 51, Madison had emphasized that "If men were angels, no government would be necessary," nor would external or internal controls be necessary. Maritain and Tocqueville knew that men are not angels. They knew that a restraining force was necessary, but they also believed that institutions could not restrain sufficiently, that it was the "habits of the heart," a democracy's culture that was more important than its institutions.

Thus, Maritain and Tocqueville would take exception with Madison's remark about the Athenian assembly. For if Athens had been peopled by Socrates-like individuals, Maritain and Tocqueville would claim that the Athenian assembly would have made better decisions than those that were actually made at the time of the Peloponnesian War. The restraining force that is a necessity for a democracy must be an independent force, that is, must come from outside of the society. Maritain mirrored Tocqueville:

> Let us understand that in order to enjoy its privileges as an adult in
> political life without running the risk of failure a people must be able to
> act grown-up: then we will understand that this era has still not passed
> when for democracy itself force—righteous force—aside from its
> normal role in the policing of societies, must also play a subsidiary role
> of protecting against the return of the instinct of domination,
> exploitation or anarchic egoism. And above all we will understand that,
> with a view to curtailing as much as possible and eliminating by
> degrees those subsidiary functions of force, more than ever democracy
> needs the evangelical ferment in order to be realized and in order to
> endure. The lasting advent of the democratic state of mind and of the
> democratic philosophy requires the energies of the Gospel to penetrate
> secular existence, taming the irrational to reason and becoming in the
> vital dynamism of the tendencies and instincts of nature, in order to
> fashion and stabilize in the depths of the subconscious those reflexes,
> habits, and virtues without which the intellect, which leads action,
> fluctuates with the wind, and wasting egoism prevails in man.[9]

Tocqueville, Maritain, and Madison had put their fingers on what has
been the perceived weakness of democracy. The people, according to
Plato, for example, are ruled by the passions of the moment. They are
consumed with immediate gratification for their self-interests. Socrates, in
The Republic, described democratic man as living from day to day
indulging in his various appetites. Democratic man's "life has neither law
nor order; and this distracted existence he terms joy and bliss and
freedom; and so he goes on."[10]

Unbridled self-interest is the hallmark of both the anarchic and
bourgeois liberal democracies that Maritain saw as the ruin of Western
culture. These democracies had been taken over by self-interest as the
only true basis of human conduct through the well-publicized writings of
socialist or romantic writers of the nineteenth century, resulting in the
spread of rational egoism throughout Western Europe. A paradigm of that
type of thinking was the Rousseauistic romantic, Nikolai Chernyshevsky,
whose philosophy of self-interest dominated Russian intellectualism. In a
seminal work, ostensibly a novel, *What Is To Be Done?*, Chernyshevesky
created an intellectual foundation for the Soviet "utopia" of the twentieth
century.

Chernyshevesky's avatar was Rousseau, whose novel *Julie ou la
nouvelle Heloise*, published in 1761 "served as one of Chernyshevsky's
most important sources."[11] Rousseau's heroine, Julie d'Etange was the

model for Chernyshevsky's, Julie Leteiller, "the semi-liberated French courtesan who acts as a foil for the heroine, Vera Pavlona."[12] Indeed, Vera Pavlona is a "new 'improved' version of Rousseau's Julie."[13] Chernyshevsky's male heroes, Lopukhov and Kirsanov, exemplify the new socialist-romantic man, the individual motivated by "rational egoism." In the following colloquy between Lopukhov and Vera Pavlona, Lopukhov exalts rational egoism:

> But must one view life in that way? (these were the first words Marya Aleksevna overheard).
>
> Yes Vera Pavlona, one must.
>
> In other words these cold and practical people are telling the truth when they say that man is governed exclusively by the calculation of his own advantage?
>
> Yes, they are telling the truth. What we call sublime emotion or ideal aspiration-all that, in the general course of life, is completely insignificant in comparison with each person's pursuit of his own advantage. And in essence these things constitute the same pursuit of advantage.[14]

Maritain and Tocqueville rejected the type of morality exemplified by Chernyshevsky. They saw unbridled self-interest as the bane of democracy just as Plato and the classical critics of democracy claimed. Tocqueville noted that self-interest in a body politic increased in direct proportion to the increase in equality. In a democracy where all are equal, all fervently pursue their self interest.[15] Christianity combated this excessive individualism.

> But whilst man takes delight in this honest and lawful pursuit of his well-being, it is to be apprehended that he may in the end lose the use of his sublimest faculties; and that whilst he is busied in improving all around him, he may at length degrade himself. Here and here only does the peril lie. It should therefore be the unceasing object of the legislators of democracies, and of all the virtuous and enlightened men who live there, to raise the souls of their fellow-citizens, and keep them lifted up towards Heaven. . . . If amongst the opinions of a democratic people any of those pernicious theories exist which tend to inculcate that all perishes with the body, let men by whom such theories are professed be marked as the natural foes of such a people.[16]

Tocqueville in language remarkably similar to that of Maritain a century later, continued that while materialism is a "dangerous disease of the human mind; but it is more especially to be dreaded among a democratic people. . . ."[17] Because democracy encourages self-interest, men living in a democratic society "believe that all is matter only."[18] Religion, according to Tocqueville, must be cultivated in a democracy. Religion gives to democratic man "a lofty cast to their opinions and their tastes, and to bid them tend with no interested motive, as it were by impulse, to pure feelings and elevated thoughts."[19] It was particularly important for democracies that "spiritual opinions should prevail." Tocqueville was absolutely convinced that Christianity must "be maintained at any cost in the bosom of modern democracies. . . ."[20]

In Maritain's terms, the democratic man that Socrates described was consumed with matter, he lacked a spiritual core. For Maritain, as for Tocqueville, given democracy's stress on liberty and equality, the only way to combat the inherent moral looseness of a democratic society is through Christianity. This is the "deepest principle of the democratic ideal, which is the secular name for the ideal of Christianity."[21] As noted above, for Maritain it is Christianity that moderates democratic man's rapaciousness by imposing on him the admonition, "Do not seek your own interests, but rather that of others. Lest what was seen in Christ Jesus be seen in you."[22]

Tocqueville noted that in the American democracy because of the self-restraining influence of Christianity "the human mind is never left to wander across a boundless field; and whatever may be its pretensions, it is checked from time to time by barriers which it cannot surmount." Tocqueville observed that because of Christianity "every principle of the moral world is fixed and determinate, although the political world is abandoned to the debates and experiments of men." In the field of morality before "the human mind" in conjunction with the will can generate destructive and immoral acts, the "certain primal and immutable principles" of Christianity acts as check on the "boldest conceptions of human device," which are "subjected to certain forms which retard and stop their completion."[23]

Tocqueville agreed with Maritain's contention that Christianity has a symbiosis with democracy. The colonists brought to the New World "a form of Christianity which I cannot better describe, then by styling it a democratic and republican religion." Christianity "contributed powerfully to the establishment of democracy in America." After the initial founding of the American nation, "politics and religion contracted an alliance which has never been dissolved."[24]

In *Reflections on America* written in 1958, Maritain noticed that this "alliance" commented on by Tocqueville was still alive. Maritain perceived Americans as "bruised souls," bruised from the travails of leaving a fatherland because of persecution and prejudice and coming to America. The bruises, according to Maritain, are evangelical in nature, a "spark of the Gospel lying deep in people who more often than not do not think at all of the Gospel." The spark is "hidden in the secret life of souls, and covered by all the ordinary selfish desires and concerns of human nature. . . . There is in the existential sense, a strain of Gospel fraternal love deep in the American blood."[25] Because of this largely hidden strain of the gospel Maritain concluded that America was not a bourgeois nation. He saw the America of the late 1950s as having the potential to become a personalist or Christian-inspired democracy. He had earlier remarked in *Man and the State* that the United States Constitution could be "described as an outstanding lay Christian document" tinged with the philosophy of the day. He continued that:

> The spirit and inspiration of this great political Christian document is basically repugnant to the idea of making human society stand aloof from God and any religious faith. Thanksgiving and public prayer, the invocation of the name of God at the occasion of any major official gathering, are, in the practical behavior of the nation, a token of this same spirit and inspiration.[26]

In *Reflections On America*, he quoted the foregoing passage from *Man and the State* and opined that the founding fathers were not meta-physicians or theologians. Nevertheless, their "philosophy of life, and their political philosophy, their notion of natural law and of human rights were permeated with concepts worked out by Christian reason and backed up by an unshakable religious feeling."[27] Maritain was aware of the First Amendment's prohibition of mixing of church and state. Yet he thought that the practical application of the amendment resulted in a society where Christian principles could exercise a moral power. Maritain noted an antagonistic secular force in America, but he doubted that this negative force would be able to loosen America's Christian underpinning.[28] Subsequent events proved him mistaken as America developed into a culture where competing self-interests constantly battled each other.

Democracy and Christianity work hand in glove in restraining self-interest because, as Tocqueville also noted, in a democracy, the people make the laws and therefore are motivated to respect what they themselves have made. The people will adhere more to the spirit of a law than to its letter which may have lacunae.[29] The people are also guided by the morality of Christianity so that the laws reflect this morality and the people are restrained by the morality to observe the spirit of the laws and to observe a morality that goes beyond the laws.

Tocqueville thought that Roman Catholicism was not the natural enemy of democracy as had been supposed by the conventional wisdom of the day. Quite the contrary. He pointed out that the Catholic Church has only two classes—priests and lay persons. In certain matters of religion, not all, the priests are above the laity, otherwise all are equal. The same morality applies to "the wise and the ignorant, the man of genius and the vulgar crowd . . . the rich and the needy, it afflicts the same austerities upon the strong and the weak . . . it confounds all the distinctions of society at the foot of the same altar, even as they are confounded in the sight of God."[30]

In the passage from *Christianity and Democracy* quoted above, Maritain was referring to the mutual dependency of Christianity and democracy. Christianity restrains ruled and the rulers. The rulers are restrained from acting corruptly in derogation of the common good. The restraint goes beyond inhibiting self-interest, promoting a negative type of freedom. Christianity also fosters a positive freedom—through the gospel that preaches the brotherhood of man. Christian charity and friendship form a culture that forges the social bond that binds the diverse elements that comprise the body politic.

FELLOWSHIP AND COMMUNITY

"So I tell you to love one another;" "Regarding brotherly love, have love for one another."[31] Maritain took Christ's command as the defining principle for a political order. For Maritain, religion—specifically Christianity—must permeate and energize the body politic and Christian charity is the actualization of Christianity in a democracy's body politic. Tocqueville agreed. He noted that "hardly any human action . . . does not originate in some very general idea men have conceived of the Deity, of His relation to mankind, of the nature of their souls, and of their duties toward their fellow creatures."[32] It was man's duty to his fellow creatures that Maritain and Tocqueville saw must be the ground for a democratic political order.

Subsumed within the Christian concept of charity is fellowship, which, for Maritain:

connotes something positive—positive and elementary—in human relationships. It conjures up the image of traveling companions, who meet here below by chance and journey through life—however fundamental their differences may be—good humoridly, in cordial solidarity and human agreement, or better to say, friendly and cooperative disagreement.[33]

In an essay "To Exist with the People" Maritain was even more explicit about what he considered the fundamentals of Christian Charity. "To exist with" is an ethical concept. It means more than a sentimental desire to do good. It is not impersonal. To exist with "does not mean to live with someone in the physical sense, or in the same way as he lives;" nor does it mean wishing someone well. It means "becoming one with him, of bearing his burdens, of living a common moral life with him, of feeling with him, and suffering with him."[34]

Maritain specifically rejected Rousseauistic pity or compassion as basis for man's duty to his fellow men. Rousseauistic compassion is the ground for a naiveté that expresses itself in a general and sentimental love of humanity. The modern thinker who critically analyzed this flawed type of caring for one's neighbor was Irving Babbitt, who called it sentimental humanitarianism.[35]

Dostoevsky provided a glimpse of sentimental humanitarian thinking in *Crime and Punishment* when Lebezyatnikov justified Sonia's prostitution:

> In my opinion, that is according to my personal conviction, it is the most normal condition for a woman. . . . In our present society it is not, of course entirely normal, because it is forced on her, but in the future it will be completely normal, because freely chosen. And even now she had the right to act as she did; she was suffering, and that was her stock, so to speak, her capital, which she had a perfect right to dispose of. Of course in the future society there will be no need of capital funds; but her role will be given a different significance, under harmonious and rational conditions. As for Sonia Semenovana herself, in present conditions, I look upon her action as a spirited protest against the organization of society and I deeply respect her for it; I rejoice to see her![36]

Distilled to its essentials the sentimental humanitarian believes that man is inherently good, that the passions and feelings are the ground for ethical action, that society is to blame for the ills of the world, and that those ills can be corrected by a feeling of universal pity for mankind coupled with corrective action in the political order—politics can cure society's ills. Sentimental humanitarianism can be allied with religious convictions as "a sort of parody of Christian charity" in that Christian charity is viewed as a form of humanitarianism.[37] The sentimental humanitarian's pity or compassion is the "sentimental desire to do good" that Maritain rejected as the basis for an organic democracy. It is sentimental humanitarianism with its impersonal compassion and pity combined with a utopian belief that the political order in the form of the State can rid the culture of the ills of mankind and create an earthly paradise that Maritain saw as the monogram of the liberal welfare state.

On the other hand, true fellowship for Maritain was rooted in Christian charity which "goes first to God, and then to all men, because the more men are loved in God and for God the more they are loved in themselves."[38] Rousseauistic pity or compassion is a lover of essences not existences. This type of compassion embraces all humanity, but as a reflection of self-love, a manifestation of man's pride, not as a manifestation of love of God. In rejecting Rousseauistic pity and the "simple human benevolence which philosophers praise," Maritain once again credited Bergson in *The Two Sources* for making clear that Christian charity can "open the heart of *all men* [Maritain's emphasis], because coming from God who first loves us, charity desires for all men the same divine good, the same eternal life, as it does ourselves. . . ."[39]

The type of friendship that Maritain had in mind as the ground for his personalist or Christian-inspired democracy is the unselfish love of neighbor demanded by the Christian Gospel. Maritain explained:

> Nor does the friendship of charity merely make us recognize the *existence* [Maritain's emphasis] of others—although as a matter of fact here is something already difficult enough for men, and something which includes everything essential. Not only does it make us recognize that another exists, not as an accident of the empirical world but as a human being who exists before God, and has the right to exist.[40]

Christian friendship is universal. It makes us recognize that all men exist as human beings. The universality of Christian friendship can be contrasted with the particularity of a friendship that, for example, only recognizes a certain racial grouping as worthy of friendship. Often the racist will treat a person of a different racial group as nonhuman, the existence of the other is denied. Through its universality, Christian friendship "helps us to purify our faith of the shell of egoism and subjectivity."[41] Maritain said that "it was impossible to exaggerate the vital importance of friendship to a democratic body politic, so little understood" by what he called the "sectarian liberalism" of the nineteenth century and by the "paganism of the present."[42] The believer, according to Maritain, and he meant the Christian, must "confess his God in social and temporal life, in the hard work of men."[43]

Maritain posited good will toward others as one of the main postulates of true friendship on which to base a democracy. He pointed out that those who despise charity also believe in what he termed "relativistic democracy," a democracy that cannot recognize truth. Maritain laid the theoretical justification for this type of democracy at the door of Hans Kelsen, who argued that "democracy implies ignorance of, or doubt about any absolute truth."[44] Kelsen used Pontius Pilate to illustrate relativistic democracy. Christ had responded to Pilate's inquiry that He had come to "bear witness to the truth." Pilate answered "What is truth?" and then gave Christ to the mob to be crucified. Kelsen argued that Pilate was being democratic. In a democracy it is up to the people to decide what the truth is at any given moment. A true democrat has no absolute values for in a democratic society mutual tolerance is supreme.[45] He who really knows truth must insist that *the truth* prevail upsetting the democratic equilibrium. The issue of relativism and democracy is discussed in greater detail in chapter 8.

Maritain rejected Kelsen's argument. Maritain saw Kelsen's view, which dominates bourgeois liberal democracy, as in opposition to the friendship that must permeate a true democracy, because for the relativist, "truth depends not on *what is* [Maritain's emphasis], but on what at each moment serves most effectively their party, their greed, or their hate."[46] The relativists also despise good will, or embrace a specious good will that varies from moment to moment. "Real, authentic good will indicates the sacred mystery which spells salvation for men and which makes it possible to say of a man that he is purely and simply good. It enables man to go out of themselves to meet their neighbors halfway."[47] Real good will is not situational, it does not subject to shift from one group to another as the political winds change.

Real good will has a steadfastness and a consistency that is lacking in relativistic good will. For Maritain the only kind of good will that has the necessary steadfastness and consistency is good will grounded on Christian charity for the love of God that is at the center of this kind of good will remains constant.

Maritain's reliance on good will can be traced back to Aristotle who saw good will as the first step in friendship, which is "the bond of the state."[48] Aristotle pointed out that good will and friendship are not synonymous for "We have good will both toward people whom we do not know, and without their knowing it, whereas we cannot have friendship under these conditions. . . ."[49] Maritain went further than Aristotle. Good will and friendship are part of the Christian command to love one's neighbor. So that good will and friendship are to be extended even to those that we do not know personally. Maritain like Aristotle saw friendship as not only a necessary part of the good life, but friendship is the glue that binds the democratic state together.

Friendship imbued with Christian charity leads to what Aristotle called concord, which occurs "when the citizens are of one mind concerning what is expedient—that is to say, when they make a deliberate choice of the same things or when they carry out their common resolves." Concord is concerned with practical issues, the day-to-day governance of a state. Concord does not mean that all of the citizens have the same opinions about everything.[50] Aristotle recognized that concord, which he defined as a "friendship between citizens," can only exist between "good men, since they are of one mind both with themselves and with one another." "Good" in the sense that the citizens have a common moral charter that establishes a direction, an end, for the body politic. The citizens who have concord are also "of one mind among themselves" because they have attained at least a minimum level of self-control; they are not subject to total control by the passions of the moment. This is part of the steadfastness and consistency with which Maritain was concerned. Aristotle continued that the good have concord "for good men's wishes are steadfast, and do not ebb and flow like the tide, and they wish for just and expedient ends, which they strive to attain in common."[51]

Concord does not guarantee a conflict free society. For Maritain concord means that the citizens are favorably disposed toward each other. That when they do disagree, the disagreement is without rancor or personal bitterness toward the other. Concord fosters a spirit of community. It leads to the citizens vibrating in unison together. Concord means that the citizens approach issues with an open mind; that each side can see what is good in the other's position; that they cooperate toward finding solutions that truly benefit the common good. Concord helps people who differ on issues to compromise their differences. Concord is opposed to the atomization of society and the plenary status of unbridled self-interest. Friendship and good will help to fight the conglomeration of self-interests that Madison called factions in *Federalist* 10. Those who are motivated by unbridled self-interest are incapable of concord, according to Aristotle, and Maritain would agree:

> except in some small degree, as they are of friendship, since they try to get more than their share of advantages, and take less than their share of labours and public burdens. And while each desires this for himself, he spies on his neighbor to prevent him from doing likewise; for unless they keep watch over one another, the common interests go to ruin. The result is discord, everybody trying to make others do their duty, but refusing to do it themselves.[52]

Again for Maritain the only leaven that can moderate the inherent rapaciousness of a democratic society is Christianity. It is Christianity that teaches moderation in the accumulation of material goods; it is the Christian social gospel that teaches the brotherhood of man; it is Christianity that teaches man to put his neighbor's interest before his own.

Tocqueville noted the critical significance of concord in a democratic society. He noted that in an aristocracy, "the outward intercourse of men is subject to settled conventional rules. The mores of the dominant class set the standard for all." However, as the "distinctions of rank are obliterated" there are no set standards that govern man's relations with each other.[53] In America, the citizen "does not think himself bound to pay particular attention to any of his fellow-citizens; nor does he require such attentions from them towards himself." Yet, Tocqueville also found a conflicting tendency against the aloofness described above. He noted that the equality of conditions of a democracy also tends to breed friendship and a certain level of the concord that Maritain considered so essential.

Tocqueville found a "general compassion for the members of the human race" among Americans. They do not inflict "useless ills" on each other; they are "happy to relieve the grief of others when they can do so without much hurting themselves; they are not disinterested, but they are humane."[54] Tocqueville saw the tendency toward aloofness as part of the movement that he and Maritain saw as the critical weakness of democracy—the tendency to atomization and unbridled individualism, which for Maritain are the signets of perverted democracies.

Maritain was aware of the differences in friendship. He did not expect the Christian to love everybody to the same degree. He did expect the Christian to have a basic love for all in the Christian sense. He was aware that the gospel teaching of the brotherhood of man did not come easy. He expected the Christian to work at actualizing Christ's command in the body politic:

> Civic Friendship, which is a profane image of brotherly love, is, in the
> same way, not an original state, granted ready-made; it is something to
> be conquered ceaselessly and at the price of great difficulties. It is the
> work of virtue and sacrifice, and in this sense it is that we behold
> therein the heroic ideal of such a [personalist or Christian-inspired]
> democracy.[55]

It is only Christianity that can provide a democracy with the kind of
friendship Maritain envisioned as necessary, universal in its application,
consistent in practice, that for Maritain and Tocqueville compliment and
vivify the culture and the culture's moral charter.

JUSTICE AND FRIENDSHIP

It is his emphasis on Christian friendship and charity as the ordering
principle of a democracy that accounts for the paucity of Maritain's
writings on justice. Maritain clearly saw that a theory of justice has little
meaning unless it is undergirded by friendship and Christian charity.
Justice is a natural virtue with prudence, fortitude, and temperance. None
of the natural virtues can be fully developed "without the love of charity.
To arrive at their full state of virtue, the natural moral virtues must be
united to charity. . . ."[56] Maritain recognized the importance of justice to
the body politic, but it is "natural justice" that the body politic should be
centered on, e.g. justice not dependent on the society's positive law or
some abstract model grounded on rational individuals who supposedly
will recognize it is to their advantage to have a just society, as has been
suggested, for example, by John Rawls.[57] Maritain saw the Rawlesian type
of justice deteriorating into the rational egoism of the Chernyshevsky
type.

Maritain's natural justice flows from brotherly friendship which
vivifies his democratic political order. Again Maritain followed Aristotle:

> Moreover, friendship appears to be the bond of the state; and lawgivers
> seem to set more store by it than they do by justice, for to promote
> concord, which seems akin to friendship, is their chief aim, while
> faction, which is enmity, is what they are most anxious to banish. And
> if men are friends, there is no need of justice between them; whereas
> merely to be just is not enough—a feeling of friendship also is
> necessary. Indeed the highest form of justice seems to have an element

of friendly feeling in it.[58]

The element of "friendly feeling" in justice is for Maritain Christian charity. He described this kind of friendship as the "very life-giving form" of justice. Friendship "tends toward a really human and freely achieved communion. It lives on the devotion of the human persons and their gift of themselves. They are ready to commit their existence, their possession and their honor for its sake."[59]

Tocqueville is the bridge between Aristotle and Maritain. Tocqueville noted that as a democratic body politic intensifies its pursuit of material pleasure, the society collapses into a brutish state. There is a "closer tie than is commonly supposed between the improvement of the soul and the amelioration of what belongs to the body." The relationship between soul and body cannot be ignored.[60] The effects of this relationship on a democratic society is magnified:

> If the social condition of a people, under these circumstances [pursuit of material things], becomes democratic, the danger which I here point out is thereby increased. When every one is constantly striving to change his position,—when an immense field for competition is thrown open to all,—when wealth is amassed or dissipated in the shortest possible space of time amidst the turmoil of democracy, visions of sudden and easy fortune—of great possessions easily won and lost,—of chance under all its forms,—haunt the mind. The instability of society itself fosters the natural instability of man's desires. In the midst of these perpetual fluctuations of his lot, the present grows upon his mind, until it conceals futurity from his sight, and his looks go no further than the morrow.[61]

Tocqueville continued that in the democracies that are irreligious, the philosophers and the leaders must constantly direct the body politic away from materiality for "it is only by resisting a thousand petty selfish passions of the hour, that the general and unquenchable passion for happiness can be satisfied.[62] Bergson also noted the special relationship between matter and spirit in *The Two Sources*. Maritain praised the last chapter of the book, called "Mechanics and Mysticism" for pointing out "that far from being opposites by nature [matter and spirit] attract each other and require the completion of the one by the other."[63]

In rule by Aquinas's virtuous one, for example, the imposition of spiritual values is directed from above. The same for an aristocracy of the virtuous few. In both of these regimes, the ruled can be channeled towards the spiritual, a spiritual tone can be set for the society. In a democracy, on the other hand, where the many rule and the hallmark of the regime is liberty and equality, the guiding hand of the virtuous one or few is not available. However, the expanding force of matter sets the stage for the development of a spiritual reaction.

What makes the clash of matter and spirituality so important in a democracy is that it is a spontaneous clash in contrast to a materiality being imposed from above as in the Soviet autocracy. In the former Soviet empire matter and spirituality also fed off of each other. Despite the official repression and persecution the Russian Orthodox Church and the Polish Catholic Church flourished. In a democracy it is the many who are consumed with matter, which is not forced on them. It is this spontaneous clash that Tocqueville noticed and that Bergson and Maritain agreed had to be combated. For the three thinkers the only way that a democracy can resist the movement toward materiality is for being to become other directed—to have genuine love of neighbor. Being as action must interact with other beings. Political society naturally results from the interactions. But, the actions-reactions must be leavened by the social gospel of Christianity. If not, then the forces of materiality which are inherently present in a democracy control the body politic. The result is the atomistic bourgeois liberal or anarchic democracy, followed by some form of autocracy, probably an autocracy of the technocrat or the bureaucrat.

CHRISTIAN EQUALITY

The last element in the symbiosis between Christianity and democracy is the Christian doctrine that all men are equal. Equality is, of course, one of the defining characteristics of a democracy. The effects of equality on a democracy's culture were well documented by Tocqueville. Christianity's effect on democratic equality has been woven into the foregoing discussion of its symbiosis with democracy. Maritain emphasized that the Christian doctrine that all are created by the same God and that all are equal before God gave an evangelical foundation to classical democracy, a foundation that was lacking in the Athenian and other pre-Christian democracies. After the birth of Christ there was no inherent valid warrant for denying to the many the right of self-governance in the political arena. Maritain's position that no one, even the virtuous one or the virtuous few, have an inherent right to rule, a position that he contended is mandated by Christianity, gradually developed from several sources, as noted above.

The linchpin for Maritain's contention is the Christian doctrine of the brotherhood of man.

Maritain saw this doctrine as confirming and emphasizing:

> the concrete sense of equality in nature by affirming its historical and genealogical character, and by teaching that here we are concerned with a blood relationship, properly so-called, all men being descended from the same original parents, and being brothers in Adam before they are brothers in Christ. Heirs of the same sin and the same weaknesses, but heirs also of the same original greatness, all created in the image of God and all allied to the same supernatural dignity as adopted sons of God.[64]

Since all are equal, all must have the opportunity to fully participate in the political process. Hence Maritain's early espousal of universal suffrage.

Maritain noted two fundamental philosophical errors concerning equality. The first he called the empiricist error. His empiricists, however, were not the usual "Bacon, Locke, Bentham, or John Stuart Mill," but, instead the "cheap Nietzschean, Machiavellianist, rightist-Hegalian or rightist-positive leaders of modern politics; . . ." The second philosophical error Maritain called the idealist error. It did not include "Plato, Descartes, Berkeley or Kant," but "cheap Rousseauist, enlightenmentist, Tolstoyan, left-Hegalian or leftist positivist leaders of modern politics."[65]

The empiricist error takes the natural social inequality that exists in all men, which Maritain recognized, and constructs an authoritarian political order on the superiority of an alleged master race or some other accidental inequality between men. Maritain called the empiricist error a "philosophy of enslavement." This skewed philosophy has little relevance to a theory of democracy since historically it has been manifested in totalitarian regimes such as the Third Reich of Adolf Hitler, although the empiricist error may be developed and be nurtured in a democracy. The idealist error, on the other hand, has been the ground for a welfare state democracy wherein the people rule theoretically and autocratically with a goal of absolute egalitarianism:

> The instinctive tendencies and the flame of sin which underlie this error of the spirit are a hatred of all superiority, collective envy and resentment, a thirst to impose punishment on others for the setbacks and humiliations one has suffered and the sense of guilt which burdens one. . . .

> The first consequence of the principle thus defined is the rejection—
> not only theoretical but practical—of natural inequalities. All natural
> privileges and all the privileges of the mind must be rigorously
> levelled. . . . There is room neither for the poet nor the contemplator in
> an egalitarian world. Culture as such must be flattened out.[66]

Christianity does not mandate absolute egalitarianism. "It is because
the Christian conception of life is based upon so broad, and fruitful a
certainty of the equality and community of nature between men" that
Christianity "insists so forcefully" on what Maritain called the "orderings
and hierarchies" which are at the root of the natural community of men
"and on the particular inequalities" which are necessarily involved in this
natural community.[67] Christianity not only respects these natural
inequalities, but "it furthers them, favors them, for as long as they remain
normal" these natural inequalities "lend variety to human life and
intensify the richness of life's encounters." The natural inequalities do not
hamper the natural unity of the civil community. When Maritain speaks of
these natural inequalities remaining "normal" he is referring to their
perverted use—using them as a means of exclusion. [68] Maritain saw the
differences, the inherent inequalities of human beings, as a reflection of
the various potentialities of the human being.

Maritain noted that idealistic egalitarianism interprets the word
equality "on a plane surface. . . . Equality is a profound thing—organic,
intensive, and qualitative. Let us not say that one man is as good as
another; that is a nihilistic formula which requires real meaning from deep
religious pessimism. . . ." Maritain believed that social inequality is
justified and must be proportional:

> It is also just and equitable that individuals should receive in
> proportion not to their needs or desires, which tend to become infinite,
> but to the necessities of their life and development, the means of
> putting to us their natural gifts. In this sense the more a man has, the
> more he should receive. The same care that men bestow upon their rare
> plants or their most beautiful stallions they do not bestow upon the
> superior persons who are an honor to their own species.[69]

Maritain conceived that a democracy could help alleviate social
inequalities in two ways: (1) that all social inequalities be open; that is
that there be free and easy movement from one social condition to
another; and (2) that whatever the social condition "individuals may enjoy
a state of life that is truly human and may really be able to strive (I do not

say easily, because without obstacles to override there is no progress for us) for the fullness of human development."[70] Maritain said that it was illusory to think that all may start life with socially identical opportunities. Equally illusory is the belief that the reward "of a good life should consist in a change of social level."[71] All should have the same opportunity to achieve—"each one according to his effort and his condition—their *human* [Maritain's emphasis] fullness. . . . Thus, such notions as that of equality of opportunity or equality of conditions, which egalitarianism would make chimerical, become true and proper if they are understood in the sense not of an equality pure and simple, but of *proportional* [Maritain's emphasis] equality."[72]

Maritain's personalist or Christian-inspired democracy would not be a society where absolute egalitarianism reigns. The social gospel of Christianity posits only one kind of absolute egalitarianism, which is not of the temporal world. Maritain believed that for real equality to exist in the temporal, political order, the culture of the society must be animated by "the sap of the gospel, the sense of supernatural equality of those called to a divine life, the sense of brotherly charity must permeate the temporal order to give it life and lift it up."[73]

SUMMARY

Maritain's concept of Christianity's symbiosis with democracy is grounded on the following: (1) the birth of Jesus Christ was a momentous event in the political history of the world for the Christian doctrines of the brotherhood of man and that all men were created by the same God to His image and likeness provided a religious undergirding for democracy; (2) the concept of the person, the spiritual nature of man, was fully actualized only under Christianity. This concept of personality is of theological origin rooted in the Christian doctrines of the Holy Trinity and the Incarnation and forms the ultimate foundation for the political rights of man; (3) democracy as a form of civil government is of divine origin for God the ultimate source of all authority gave to the many, the human community, the right and the power to govern themselves.

Tocqueville's empirical observations of the American democracy of the 1830s were meant to be, and have proven to be, valid for democracies in general. Those observations demonstrate that democracy more than any other form of government must have a restraining force to inhibit unbridled self-interest. A democratic society with its inherent tendency toward atomization and individualism must have a moral charter and the relationship and duties of democratic citizens toward each other must be based on something that transcends positive law. For Maritain and Tocqueville the transcendental force that vivifies and animates a democratic body politic must be Christianity, which is the only force that is consistent, universal, and that actually teaches unselfishness and love of one's fellow man. Without the leaven of the Christian social gospel, democracy will invariably disintegrate into an atomistic society that Maritain called bourgeois liberalism, or into an autocracy of the people where the technocrat or the bureaucrat are supreme.

With the basics of the Christianity-democracy symbiosis in place, this study now turns to the practical workings of Maritain's Christian-inspired democracy.

NOTES

1. *Democracy in America*, lxxxi-lxxxvii.
2. Ibid., 33-34.
3. In Alexis de Tocqueville, "Letter to Claude-François de Corcelle," Saint-Cyr, près Tours, September 17, 1853, *Selected Letters on Politics and Society*, ed. Roger Boesche, trans. James Toupin and Roger Boesche (Berkeley, California: University of California Press, 1985), 292-294.
4. Ibid.
5. Alexis de Tocqueville, *The Recollections of Alexis deTocqueville*, ed. and intro. by J. P. Mayer, trans. Alexander Teixeira De Mattos (Morningside Heights, New York: Columbia University Press, 1949).
6. Letter to Corcelle, 294.
7. *Democracy in America*, vol. I, 362.
8. *The Federalist*, No. 55 (J. Madison).
9. *Christianity and Democracy*, 53.
10. Plato *The Republic*, VIII, 559d-562a (Jowett translation).
11. Nikolai Chernyshevsky, *What Is To Be Done?*, trans. by Michael R. Katz, annotated by William G. Wagner (Ithaca, New York: Cornell University Press, 1989) 23. The quotation is from Katz's and Wagner's Introduction.
12. Ibid.
13. Ibid.
14. *What Is To Be Done?* at 115.

15. *Democracy in America*, II, chaps. II, III, and IV.

16. Ibid., II, 172.

17. Ibid., 173.

18. Ibid.

19. Ibid., 174.

20. Ibid., 175.

21. *Christianity and Democracy*, 54.

22. Philippians 2:4-5. See also Matthew 25.

23. *Democracy in* America, I, 361.

24. *Democracy in America*, I, 355.

25. *Reflections on America*, 85-86.

26. *Man and the State*, 183-184.

27. *Reflections on America*, 182-183.

28. Ibid.

29. *Democracy in America*, Vol. I, 289-291.

30. Ibid., 356.

31. John xv: 17; Romans xiii, 10.

32. *Democracy in America*, Vol. II, 22.

33. Jacques Maritain, *Truth and Human Fellowship* (Princeton: Princeton University Press, 1957), 21.

34. *The Range of Reason*, 121.

35. Irving Babbitt, *Democracy and Leadership* (Indianapolis, Indiana: Liberty Fund, Inc., 1979); Irving Babbitt, *Rousseau and Romanticism*, new introduction Claes Ryn (New Brunswick, New Jersey: Transaction Publishers, 1991); Peter J. Stanlis, "Babbitt, Burke and Rousseau," *Irving Babbitt in Our Time*, eds. George A. Panichas and Claes Ryn (Washington, D.C.: Catholic University of America Press, 1986), 127.

36. Fyodor Dostoevsky, *Crime and Punishment*, trans. Jessie Coulson, 2nd ed. (New York: W. W. Norton & Company, 1974), 311.

37. *Democracy and Leadership*, 74.

38. *Truth and Human Fellowship*, 26.

39. *Ransoming the Time*, 124.

40. *Truth and Human Fellowship*, 26.

41. Ibid., 27.

42. *Ransoming the Time*, 128.

43. Ibid., 130.

44. *Truth and Human Fellowship*, 5; Ransoming the Time, 135.

45. *Truth and Human Fellowship*, 6.

46. *Ransoming the Time*, 135.

47. Ibid.

48. *Nichomachean Ethics*, VIII.

49. Ibid., IX.

50. *Nichomachean Ethics*, bk. IX, ch. vi.

51. Ibid.

52. Ibid.

53. *Democracy in America*, II, 204.

54. Ibid., 199.

55. *Scholasticism and Politics*, 109.

56. Ibid., 228

57. John Rawls, *A Theory of Justice* (Cambridge: Harvard University Press, 1971).

58. *Nicomachean Ethics*, VIII.

59. *Man and the State*, 10.

60. *Democracy in America*, II, 176.

61. Ibid., II, 179.

62. Ibid., II, 180.

63. *Ransoming the Time*, 89.

64. *Ransoming the Time*, 19.

65. Ibid., 2.

66. *Ransoming the Time*, 13-14.

67. Ibid., 20.

68. Ibid.

69. Ibid., 24.

70. Ibid., 27.

71. Ibid.

72. Ibid., 27-28.

73. Ibid., 31.

CHAPTER 7

THE PRACTICAL OPERATION OF MARITAIN'S DEMOCRACY

How would Maritain's personalist or Christian-inspired democracies work in the rough and tumble world of practical politics? A critical part of the answer to that question is how Maritain viewed the relationship between politics and morality and how Maritain proposed to resolve conflict among the citizens of his democracy. Would the citizens imbued with Christian charity and friendship in a culture permeated with religious values be willing to "turn the other cheek" to the extent that the political order could not function? His solution to political conflict was to wholeheartedly adopt the techniques of creative nonviolence as developed in India by Mahatma Gandhi, who like Maritain wanted to purify politics of what both thinkers perceived to be its amorality.[1] Their common objective sprang from a common source, for Gandhi was profoundly influenced by the social and political gospel of Jesus Christ.[2] Maritain and Gandhi did not believe that politics could be segregated from morality, for everything that man is and does in this world is, or should be, infused with morality. A politics stripped of morality is not politics, but an aberration of politics.[3]

Further, according to Maritain, a politics stripped of morality can have grave practical consequences. Such a politics can "bring great misfortunes in the life of peoples if instead of acting as consubstantial with politics [morality] tries to act on it from without, i.e., in a word by imposing in such a case on a politics that is *amoral*, moral rules that are *apolitical* [Maritain's emphasis]."[4] Maritain and Gandhi believed that it was impossible to be moral in private life and immoral or amoral in political life. The two spheres cannot be separated:

> I could not be leading a religious life unless I identified myself with the
> whole of mankind, and that I could not do unless I took part in politics.

> The whole gamut of man's activities today constitutes an indivisible
> whole. You cannot divide social, economic, political and purely
> religious work into watertight compartments.[5]

Maritain praised Gandhi's theory of *satyagraha*[6] as a means of "spiritual warfare" to implement direct action in the political and social sphere. Maritain tied Gandhi's theory of non-violent resistance to the Christian virtue of courage. There are two kinds of courage, "the courage that attacks and the courage that endures, the force of aggression and the force of patience. . . . opposing evil through attack and coercion—a way which, at the last extremity, leads to the shedding, if need be, of the blood of others; and opposing evil through suffering and enduring. . . ."[7] Maritain believed that the second type of courage is the Christian way.

Maritain opined that the techniques of *satyagraha* could be applied in three areas of political activity: (1) the struggle against colonialism; (2) the struggle of citizens to gain control over their state; and (3) the struggle "of Christians to transform civilization by making it actually Christian, actually inspired by the Gospel." These comments reflect Maritain's belief, never expressly stated, that Christians could and should resort to Gandhi's nonviolent techniques to achieve political objectives in the western democracies. The pinnacle of the Christian's political objectives was to actualize a Christian-inspired democracy.[8] Maritain criticized the Christian Democratic parties of the post-World War II era for neglecting Gandhi's teaching on direct political action as a means of transforming European society at that time.

It was against the oppressive power of the state's bureaucracy that Maritain thought Gandhi's techniques would be most effective. "The spiritual means of political warfare can provide the people with a supreme weapon to get or keep control not only of their government, but also of that big, anonymous machinery itself."[9] Maritain gave practical meaning to his words when he supported and inspired one of Gandhi's American disciples, Saul Alinsky, who used Gandhi's nonviolent techniques against the Chicago city bureaucracy. Alinsky and Maritain met while Maritain was teaching at the University of Chicago.[10] Maritain regarded Alinsky's work in the stockyard area of Chicago as an example of integral or theocentric humanism at work, "where for generations ethnic hatreds and rivalries had mocked Christian teaching," as an opportunity for "renewed spirituality and democratic citizenship."[11]

Despite the conflation of their political philosophies, Maritain did not completely accept Gandhi's theory of nonviolence. Maritain did not condemn, "like Gandhi, any recourse to force (carnal force, force of coercion)." Like Gandhi, Maritain believed that the means employed in the political order were important.[12] Iyer, Gandhi's political biographer, makes this comparison:

> The closest approximation to Gandhi's view of the means-end relationship is that of Jacques Maritain who regards the problem of End and Means as *the* [Iyer's emphasis] basic problem of political philosophy. . . . It is a universal and inviolable axiom for Maritain, an obvious primary principle, that "means must be proportionate and appropriate to the end since they are the ways to the end and, so to speak, the end itself in its very process of coming into existence. So that applying intrinsically evil means to attain an intrinsically good end is simply nonsense and a blunder."

Iyer traces Gandhi's and Maritain's conflation of means and ends "not merely" to their rejection of utilitarianism, "but also because of their daringly unorthodox repudiation of the so-called pragmatist view of politics and the dominant doctrine of double standards" that differentiate between individual conduct and the conduct of public officials.[13]

The two thinkers differed in that Maritain was more willing than Gandhi to accept the realities of politics; that at times political leaders have to do things that in the nonpolitical context would be morally condemned. Force was one means among many, one that Maritain was not willing to categorically rule out. He conceded that the use of force "poses a problem for the Christian, a problem all the more grave," since even just force is "charged with sorrow and with sin." Political leaders, according to Maritain, "are not only bound to impose with the bridle of justice on means which come from the world of wild beasts, and to reject in an absolute manner the use of force as a means of persuasion or as a means of facility."[14]

THE PROPHETIC-SHOCK MINORITY

Maritain undoubtedly saw Gandhi as one of the paradigmatic individuals that Bergson wrote about in *The Two Sources of Morality and Religion*.[15] The paradigmatic individual is a morally inspired person, like Gandhi or Mother Teresa, who by the force of his or her moral example moves a democratic society toward Bergson's open or dynamic morality. Bergson saw the Christian mystics as fulfilling this role. Both Bergson and Maritain believed that a democracy requires paradigmatic individuals to guide the many away from their natural tendency toward self-interest.[16]

Maritain had adumbrated the concept of the paradigmatic individual in his prophetic-shock minority, which included individuals like Saul Alinsky in Chicago who would provoke the moral conscience of the community.

The prophetic-shock minority is an individual, or a group, whose task is to enlarge the moral charter of democracy by espousing spiritual values that have not been accepted by the majority of citizens. Maritain called this special class of persons, "inspired servants or prophets of the people."[17] They are "inspired" and "prophets," because their spiritual development is ahead of the rest of society. The prophetic-shock minority are the forerunners who are necessary for the continual moral development of a democratic society. They help to form and solidify the bonding of society by articulating values that should be included in the moral charter. "They are needed in the normal functioning" of the society, but they are especially needed "in the periods of crisis, birth, or basic renewal. . . ."[18] Maritain compared the prophetic shock minority to the "great stewards" and grand counselors who advised kings in the past. Their advice offered solutions that were novel, ahead of the perceived knowledge of the time. They were willing to take risks, to advise the king to eschew the routine, the commonplace.

> When they were mistaken, they were broken by the king, sometimes they were sent into exile or they were hanged. . . . In democratic societies the people play the part of the king, and the inspired servants of the people that of the great counselors. As a rule they are prophets of emancipation—national, political, or social emancipation.[19]

Maritain mentions such diverse individuals as Thomas Jefferson, Gandhi, John Brown, and the leaders of the Italian *Risorgimento* as examples of the prophetic-shock minority.

This group can be brought into clearer focus by comparing it with a similar idea advanced by one of Maritain's contemporaries and intellectual kinsman, Peter Viereck.[20] In his book The *Unadjusted Man*, Viereck described a new type of hero:

> Today the humanist, the artist, the scholar can no longer be the prophet and seer, the unriddler of the outer universe; modern science has deprived him of that function. His new heroism, unriddling the inner universe, is to be stubbornly unadjusted toward the mechanized, depersonalized bustle outside. The Unadjusted Man is the final, irreducible pebble that sabotages the omnipotence of even the smoothest running machine. . . . Indeed he is no hero at all in the eyes of the majority, but a laughable Quixote, too unadjusted to settle down

with a steady, productive windmill. His values are not determined by a democratic plebiscite.[21]

Viereck linked the unadjusted man to Christianity in language that is a paraphrase of Maritain's concept of the person. Christianity recovers the "infinite preciousness of each individual soul" and "builds up a deep soul-felt inner shield against the outer claims of over adjustment."[22] In the body politic the prophetic-shock minority and the unadjusted man are a bulwark not only against tyranny and totalitarianism, but also against a materialistic culture generally.

Viereck and Maritain agreed that principled dissenters are needed in any political order, but particularly in the kind of a democracy where the majority can run roughshod over the minority, what Maritain called the anarchic and bourgeois liberal democracy. Viereck wrote with the greater clarity about the spiritual undergirding of this type of dissenter. There is a warrant for attributing a primarily spiritual character to the inspired servant of Maritain also, although Maritain did not explicitly link the inspired servant to Christianity. Some of his examples, i.e., Jefferson, were not known for their religious fervor, some were, i.e., Gandhi.

The purpose of the inspired servants is to move society away from the material, away from individualist democracy toward the spiritual, the personalist democracy; to *"awaken* [Maritain's emphasis] the people, to awaken them to something better than everyone's daily business, to the task of the supra-individual task to be performed."[23] Maritain continued:

> That is a quite vital and necessary social phenomenon. And it is quite a dangerous phenomenon. For where there is inspiration and prophecy, there are false prophets and true prophets; thieves aiming to dominate men and servants aiming to set them free; inspiration from dark instincts and inspiration from genuine love. And nothing is more difficult than what is called "discrimination between spirits." It is easy to mistake impure inspiration for unsullied inspiration; nay more, it is easy to slip from genuine inspiration to a corrupt one.[24]

Maritain was personally involved in the formation of such a prophetic minority. In 1952, Roberto Rossillini's movie *The Miracle* was publicly condemned by Francis Cardinal Spellman of New York. A group of Catholic writers and artists formed under the leadership of Maritain's friend, and poet, Allen Tate, and Frederick Morgan, contemplated a lawsuit against the cardinal. Maritain cautioned Tate that, "there is nothing in common between expressing one's mind on the matter, as you did, and starting a collective action which would raise the flag of a theologico-political crusade. The confusions and misunderstandings thus engendered would jeopardize from the start all the good that such a group is capable of doing."[25] Maritain had advised Morgan that the group should focus on:

> awakening in Catholic opinion a greater awareness of the importance and dignity of the values which the writer and artist serve and of free intellectual research. . . . I am convinced that the essential thing is to go ahead with creative work. The essential task is to make appreciation and love for the works of the mind penetrate more deeply into the Catholic community, and to educate it by the same token to understand better the multiplicity of views in cultural matters of Catholics equally attached to the truths involved in their faith.[26]

The prophetic-shock minority poses a conundrum for Maritain's political thought. What distinguishes such a group from the political heretic, the true prophets from the false? The distinction has more than theoretical interest. The political heretic is to be censored by public opinion, or, if necessary, by the judicial arm of the state. The prophetic-shock minority is to be given free rein to awaken the body politic. Maritain never explained how to differentiate the true prophet from the false. The major difference between the two groups is that the prophetic-shock minority awakens society to the spiritual values that vivify the moral charter. The political heretic, on the other hand, is an intellectual corrupter, a destroyer of those values.

The difference can be clouded as was illustrated by the American experience with the peace movement during the Vietnam War. Leftist and other radicals, intellectual corrupters to Maritain, comprised part of the peace movement. But Christian pacifists and members of the Catholic peace movement also were active in the opposition to the war.[27] They tried to awaken in the American public the religious and moral values that Maritain held dear, but values that arguably were opposed to the war policy of the United States. Was Father Healy a political heretic or a true prophet? There is no easy answer. The most that can be said is that the lesson that can be drawn from the American experience as far as Maritain's conception of democracy is concerned is that there is a gray area where the difference between the false prophet and the true prophet is opaque.

Maritain would let informed public opinion decide which is true and which is false. In the personalist and Christian-inspired democracies with their publics educated in spiritual values, the foundation has been laid for a discriminating, value-centered public opinion. In the anarchic and bourgeois liberal democracies, on the other hand, the danger is great that the true prophet will either be ignored or legally suppressed.

That the prophetic-shock minority is an avatar of spiritual values is also confirmed by Maritain's contention that only the anarchic and bourgeois liberal types of democracy require a special group of inspired servants. In the personalist and Christian-inspired democracies the people themselves would function as inspired servants:

> In a democracy which has come of age, in a society of free men, expert in the virtues of freedom and just in its fundamental structures, the prophetic function would be integrated in the normal and regular life of the body politic, and issue from the people themselves. In such a society inspiration would rise from the free common activity of the people in their most elementary, most humble local communities. By choosing their leaders, at this most elementary level, through a natural and experiential process, as fellow men personally known to them and deserving their trust in the minor affairs of the community, the people would grow more and more conscious of political realities and more ready to choose their leaders, at the level of the common good of the body politic, with true political awareness, as genuine deputies for them.[28]

MEANS AND ENDS

For Maritain the problem of means and ends is "*the* [Maritain's emphasis] basic problem in political philosophy."[29] The problem cannot be understood without reference to the ultimate aim of politics, which, Maritain thought was not to ensure the material prosperity of individual citizens or to "to bring about either industrial mastery over nature, or political mastery over other men."[30] The end of politics is rather "to better the conditions of human life" by working for the common good so that each person "may truly reach that measure of independence which is proper to civilized life and guarantees of work and property, political rights, civil virtues, and the cultivation of the mind." As such the end of politics is "essentially human or moral, for morality is concerned with nothing else than the true human good."[31] Intertwined with his concept of the end of politics and of the "true common good" was his acute awareness that a Christian-inspired democracy could not be hypocritical; that is claim to be grounded on the social gospel of Jesus Christ, but act in its foreign and domestic policies in a manner antithetical to the gospel.

Politics could not succeed in its end without the aid of Christianity for in order to properly accomplish its end politics must result in the "materialization of the Gospel principles in terrestrial existence and social behavior." The means to the end was critical for the means are the end itself in the process of coming into existence.[32]

Once again the political theory of Maritain and Gandhi conflate. Gandhi said about the means-end relationship, "The means may be likened to a seed, the end to a tree; and there is just the same inviolable connection between the means and the end as there is between the seed and the tree."[33]

Maritain then was one among several thinkers of his age who wanted to purify politics with considerations of morality, in Maritain's case a Christian morality. He often spoke of the need to reinvigorate the political order with a renewed Christianity. This is a canon of all of his political writings, the central theme of *Integral Humanism* and a sub-rosa theme of *Scholasticism and Politics*:

> at the same time, Christian ethics, not really carried out in the social life of the people, become in this connection . . . a universe of formulas and words; and this universe of formulas and words was in effect vasalized . . . by the real energies of this same temporal world existentially detached from Christ. Such a disorder can be cured only by a renewal of the profoundest energies of the religious conscience, arising in temporal existence.[34]

The means-end problem was at the root of what Maritain called "Machiavellianism," the idea that any means necessary to further the perceived common good were acceptable, even those acts that outside of politics would usually be considered immoral. His opposition to Machiavellianism was expressed numerous times in his political writings, but most forcefully in *The Range of Reason* in a chapter titled "The End of Machiavellianism."[35]

Maritain pointed out that perfidy, falsehood, cruelty, assassination, bad faith and every other kind of crime had existed before Machiavelli and "will exist long after his name is only a faint memory."[36] What Machiavelli did was to separate politics and morality. Prior to the "clever Florentine" those who exercised political power immorally did so, according to Maritain, "with a bad conscience—to the extent that they had a conscience." Maritain continued:

> Therefore a specific kind of unconscious and unhappy hypocrisy—that is, the shame of appearing to oneself such as one is—a certain amount of self restraint, and that deep and deeply human uneasiness which we

> experience in doing what we do not want to do, and what is forbidden
> by a law that we know to be true, prevented the crimes in question
> from becoming a rule, and provided governed peoples with a limping
> accommodation between good and evil which, in broad outline, made
> their oppressed lives, after all, livable.[37]

After Machiavelli all kinds of political leaders could justify their actions by claiming that the immoral acts were necessary for the common good of their citizens. The leader's personal morality which may be antithetical to his political actions are put "in a parenthesis; they will stoically immolate their personal morality on the altar of political good."[38]

According to Maritain, Machiavelli's (and those political practitioners who follow Machiavelli's precepts) conception of politics is grounded in his belief that all men are bad. Maritain rejected this argument. Machiavelli did not realize that the badness of men "is not radical, that this leprosy cannot destroy man's original grandeur. . . ." By man's "original grandeur" Maritain is, of course, referring to man's spiritual nature that is created by God and which participates to a greater or lesser degree in God's spirituality. Machiavelli's political horizon was limited to the temporal sphere. In contrast, Maritain believed that politics must look beyond the temporal to the eternal, for politics has a profound influence, like it or not, on the eternal, as explained previously. Because of his limited vision about politics Machiavelli was only interested in the short term, in the practical side of politics, in how man actually lives, not how man ought to live. Maritain asked why single out politics for separation from morality?; if Machiavelli was right, "such an abandonment, such a resignation would be logical also, not only for political life, but for the entire field of human life."[39] This is the "instability and internal principle of instability" of Machiavellianism. "It essentially supposes the complete eradication of moral values in the brain of the political artist as such, yet, at the same time it also supposes the actual existence and actual vitality of moral values and moral beliefs in all others."[40]

Maritain believed that it was impossible to cordon off politics from the general morality of a culture. A political order that is amoral or immoral has a corrosive affect on the total morality of the society, contaminating the culture:

> But it is impossible that the use of supramoral, that is a thoroughly
> immoral art of politics should not produce a progressive lowering and
> degeneration of moral values and moral beliefs in the common human
> life, a progressive disintegration of the inherited stock of stable

structures and customs linked with those beliefs, and finally a
progressive corruption of the ethical and social matter itself with which
this supermoral politics deals. Thus such an art wears away and
destroys its very matter, and by the same token will degenerate itself.[41]

Here again is where Maritain's and Bergson's political theory
intersect. In Maritain's words, "The first step to be taken by everyone
who wishes to act morally is to decide not to act according to the general
customs and doings of his fellow-men. This is a precept of the Gospel:
'Do not ye after their works; for they say, and do not. . . .'"[42] In other
words the open, dynamic morality of Christianity must control, not the
traditional, static morality of custom or expediency. Justice and moral
virtues cannot prevent the destruction of a society from natural causes.
However, once justice and moral virtue are corrupted by the political
leadership of the state by their embrace of Machiavellianism an "internal
principle of death is introduced into the core of society." Therefore,
according to Maritain, justice and moral virtue have a capacity in and of
themselves to foster the continuance of the body politic. Injustice and
immorality have the opposite tendency, they are the instruments of a body
politic's death.[43]

This is also the intersection of Maritain's political ontology with his
political philosophy. He would argue that Machiavellianism is ultimately
grounded on a metaphysics that exalts matter; an ontology that relegates
man's spiritual nature to a secondary role in his life in that the spiritual
nature is excluded from man's politics even though it is politics that will
have a major impact on the nourishment and growth of that spiritual
nature. Maritain could point to the ontology of Martin Heidegger as a
paradigm of an ontology that follows a straight line not only to Nazism,
but also to Machiavellianism. Is not Machiavellianism a part of "leap in"
or "leap ahead" caring? Were not the activities of the Third Reich
consistent with the teachings of *The Prince*? According to Herman
Rauschning, Hitler had read and reread *The Prince*; for a long time the
book did not leave Hitler's side.[44] Only after he had read *The Prince*,
Rauschning was told by Hitler, did he really understand politics; the book
had purged his mind of false ideas and prejudices about politics.[45]

THE COMMON GOOD

For Maritain the common good is primarily an ethical concept. It
consists of the good life, a life "both morally straight and happy. . . . The

common good is at once material, intellectual and moral, and principally moral, as man himself is; it is a common good of human persons," a common good that has "an indirect reference" to man's eternal destiny.[46] The common good transcends mere utility. Maritain was clear. Bad faith, perfidy, lying, cruelty, assassination, "and all other procedures of this kind" are injurious to the common good "and tend by themselves towards its corruption."

In practice Maritain noted two kinds of Machiavellianism. The first he called a "dignified, conservative Machiavellianism, using injustice, within 'reasonable' limits. . . ."[47] This type of Machiavellianism while injurious to the common good did not completely corrupt it, being restrained by the moral values of the culture, "or by traditions of good diplomatic form and respectability . . . or a lack of imagination, of boldness, and of inclination to take risks." Cardinal Richlieu was the leading proponent of "moderate Machiavellianism."[48]

The second kind of Machiavellianism, Maritain called "absolute Machiavellianism." Its primary intellectual progenitor was nineteenth-century positivism which "considered politics to be not a mere art, but a mere natural science, like astronomy or chemistry." Maritain regarded political positivism as much more "inhuman than Machiavelli himself."

A secondary intellectual progenitor was the German Romanticism of Fichte and Hegel with its "cult of the state."[49] The Hegelian cult of the state, according to Maritain is a "metaphysical sublimation of Machiavelli's principles. . . . Machiavellianism is no longer politics, it is metaphysics, it is a religion, a prophetic and mystical enthusiasm."[50]

Maritain admitted that absolute Machiavellianism will succeed—in the short term. "How could it not succeed, when everything has been sacrificed to the aim of success? Here is the ordeal and the scandal of contemporary conscience."[51] Maritain believed that politics must be purged of all Machiavellianism. While the purge is in progress those who oppose absolute Machiavellianism "will be able to stop its triumphs and to overcome its standard-bearers only in risking in this struggle their blood and their wealth and the dearest treasures of peaceful civilization."[52]

How was the purge to be accomplished? For Maritain this was the "great problem." A moral conscience is never allowed "to do evil for any good whatsoever." Maritain pointed out that when Satan promised Christ the world for His subservience, Christ rejected the offer. State and politics when they are separated from ethics are "the realm of those demonical principalities of which St. Paul spoke." However, Maritain was not naive. He realized that the standards of personal ethics could not be carried over into politics without some modification. He asked:

> Is Morality willing, is Christianity willing, is God willing that, of
> necessity, all our freedoms be conquered, our civilization destroyed,
> the very hope annihilated of seeing a little justice and brotherly amity
> raise our earthly life—are they willing that, of necessity, our lives be
> enslaved, our temples and institutions broken down, our brethren
> persecuted and crushed, our children corrupted, our very souls and
> intelligence delivered over to perversion by the great imperial
> standard-bearers of Machiavellianism—because of the very fact that
> we adhere to justice and refuse the devil while they dare to use
> injustice and evil and accede to the devil up to the end?[53]

Part of the answer, according to Maritain, is that the truly just man or
nation, animated by Christian morality, may have to tolerate some
existing evil as long as there "is no furthering of or cooperation with the
same." At times "even dissimulation is not always bad faith or knavery. It
would not be moral, but foolish, to open up one's heart and inner thoughts
to any dull or mischievous fellow. Stupidity is never moral, it is a vice. . .
Yet a certain amount of cunning, if it is intended to deceive evil-disposed
persons, must not be considered fox's wiles, but intellect's legitimate
weapon."[54] Maritain recognized that it is not easy to know where to draw
the line. The exigent circumstances of each situation must be assessed
separately. Maritain sanctioned the use of intelligence services, the
utilization of "corrupted people," selfishness and self-assertion, distrust
and suspicion, the recognition of the principle of the lesser evil and the
fait accompli. In certain circumstances "all of these things are in reality
ethically grounded."[55] Maritain was aware that a weak state "surrounded
and threatened" by Machiavellian enemies must increase its "physical
power," its military force, but the best way to fight Machiavellianism is
for the weak state to increase its moral virtue.[56]

The second bulwark against absolute Machiavellianism was
Maritain's belief that absolute Machiavellianism does not succeed—in the
long-term. The failure of German Romanticism and the concomitant rise
of the Third Reich, as chronicled by Friedrich Meinecke, is an example of
the long term failure of absolute Machiavellianism. It is noteworthy that
Meinecke, a participant in the events in Germany and, at one time, an
advocate of the cult of the state, realized the moral impotence of
Machiavellianism. Eventually Meinecke came to a point of view close to
Maritain's.[57]

Maritain's thesis that Machiavellianism does not succeed over the
long-term is grounded in metaphysics. "[T]he endless reserves of evil . . .
are one, in reality, the power of corruption—the squandering and
dissipation of the substance and energy of Being and of good. Such a

power destroys itself by destroying that good which is its subject." True justice and Christian morality and charity "works through its own causality toward welfare and success in the future, as a healthy sap works toward the perfect fruit, and that Machiavellianism works through its own causality for ruin and bankruptcy, as poison in the sap works for the illness and death of the tree."[58]

For Maritain, it is the long-term that must be considered in politics. Political action, instead of "hypnotizing itself on the present moment, would reckon on *duration* [Maritain's emphasis], and take into account the time of maturation necessary for an integral humanist renewal of the temporal order."[59] Maritain believed that too often, if not most of the time, politicians are only concerned with the short-term and that this tendency fosters a resort to Machiavellianism. This situation occurs most frequently in a democracy where the next election is not that far removed from the present. The political leadership of a democracy have a tendency to curry favor with the many by adopting policies that are successful in the short-term so that the leader can be reelected.

That Maritain perceived what he called the dilemma of Machiavellianism to be crucial to a democracy is beyond caveat. Democracy is the only way of bringing about what Maritain called a moral rationalization of politics because democracy is a "rational organization of freedoms founded upon law."[60] Democracy carries the highest aspiration of human beings. The dilemma for democracy is clear. "[E]ither to perish by continuing to accept, more or less willingly, the principle of Machiavellianism, or to regenerate by consciously and decidedly rejecting this principle."[61] The rejection of Machiavellianism was an important step from bourgeois liberal democracy to a Christian inspired democracy. The use by democracy of Machiavellian-type means would be suicide. According to Maritain, there is an inherent opposition between Machiavellianism and democracy, "the commonwealth of free men":

> The only Machiavellianism of which any democracy as such is capable is attenuated and weak Machiavellianism. Facing absolute Machiavellianism, either the democratic states, inheritors of the *Ancien Régime* and of its old Machiavellianism policy, will keep on using weak Machiavellianism, and they will be destroyed from without, or they will decide to have recourse to absolute Machiavellianism, which is only possible with totalitarian rule and totalitarian spirit; and thus they will destroy themselves from within. They will survive only on condition that they break with Machiavellianism in any of the forms in which it may appear.[62]

Maritain's proscription for democracy was to use force and the other means which would be considered immoral in the nonpolitical context sparingly and make the means proportional to the immediate political ends sought. What Maritain termed the "means of edification" and the "spiritual means of war" must be employed first. These are the "means of patience and voluntary suffering, which are par excellence the means of love and truth."

Maritain had a prescription for how a democracy can avoid Machiavellianism. First, a democracy must be circumspect in the use of force. It should be used only as a last resort and in limited amounts, only enough to accomplish a limited goal. As pointed out above, the use of force by a body politic raised serious moral issues for Maritain. Whenever possible force must be avoided. The other tactics of Machiavellianism, lying, bad faith, etc., should be rarely employed and only after less radical means had been tried. Maritain insisted that the means be proportional to the immediate political ends sought. He believed in a hierarchy of means; the order of means must correspond to the order of ends. An end "worthy of man should be pursued with means worthy of man." Means should be employed that are "not only good in general, but truly proportionate to their end . . . means in which that very justice which pertains to the common good and the sanctification of secular life which pertains to its perfection shall be embodied."[63]

What he called the "means of edification" and the "spiritual means of war" must be employed first, means which include patience and even voluntary suffering. As noted above, Maritain believed that a democracy must have a moral charter; this was essential for his personalist and Christian-inspired democracies. In its dealings with its citizens and in the conduct of its foreign relations, he believed that a democracy must abide by its moral charter. He was willing to allow some deviation from the moral charter, a slight deviation in domestic matters, and more deviation in foreign affairs, as called for by exigent circumstances.

A democratic society can fight the "temptation" of Machiavellianism only through the practice of a Christian politics. Mere "natural morality" or moral conscience is not enough unless it is fortified with a religious conscience. The religious conscience gives political leaders a universal outlook. It is the conscience of the dynamic morality that allows for the transcendence of the leader's vision away from provincial loyalties. "What is able to face Machiavellianism . . . is not, a just politics appealing only to the natural forces of man, it is Christian politics." The reason that this is so is that Christian politics is "mindful of the eternal destiny of man" and is a politics that recognizes and emphasizes man's spiritual nature. Christian politics is armed with the social gospel, a "real and concrete justice, with force, perspicacity and prudence."[64]

Christian politics precisely because it considers man's eternal destiny looks to the long-term; it understands what Maritain called "political duration," the real time required by "political reality to mature and fructify." "Political duration" is somewhat analogous to Bergson's duration, "the continuous life of a memory which prolongs the past into the present."[65] The moral charter of a democracy provides the ground for the democracy's political duration by giving the democracy an institutional memory with substance and experience of how the democracy applied the charter in the past; how the charter was developed by the body politic, and most importantly, the principles that are the foundation of the charter. In this way, the democracy's memory has the long-term perspective that Maritain thought necessary for a proper evaluation of current and future means and ends, as actualized in courses of action to be pursued.

Nations, states, and civilizations are subject, like all mortal things, to decay and death, not only from physical, but also from moral causes. Christian politics undermines this natural tendency to decay by developing the soul of the body politic. And for Maritain, a body politic with a soul, that is a body politic with a spiritual base, "tends to render such peoples unconquerable. If they are conquered and oppressed, they remain alive and keep on struggling under oppression."[66] As an example of the staying power of a civilization with a soul, Maritain mentioned the "house of Israel, whose internal immaterial force and principle of communion is of a supra-political and supra-temporal order."[67]

REPRESENTATION

Another idea pivotal to Maritain's democracy is representation. It is "absolutely essential to genuine democratic philosophy."[68] Rousseau's plebiscitary democracy in which theoretically the many wield political power through their personal participation in the general will was not only practically unworkable, but eventually lead to a totalitarian democracy, as set forth above. Since the many cannot participate directly, it is through their representatives that the many control their government.[69]

Representatives in a democracy are authorized or commissioned by the people to exercise authority. For Maritain, the representative is a vicar, who rules vicariously for the people, in their place. The representative exercises the authority that belongs to the people, are made by the people to "participate, to some great extent, in the authority of the people." The representative has no authority outside of that derived from the many. In vesting their representatives with authority, "the people lose in no way possession of their basic right to self-government." The authority of the representative is derivative, always incomplete and temporary, for the many, at any time, can divest the representative of authority.

Although Maritain did not use the legal word "fiduciary" in describing the many-representative relationship, that word aptly conveys how he perceived the nature of the relationship. Legally, a fiduciary is one "to whom property or power is entrusted for the benefit of another."[70] A fiduciary relationship is one grounded on trust and confidence. The law imposes a strict duty on fiduciaries to act solely for the benefit of their principals. A failure to do so exposes the fiduciary to harsh penalties, including possible criminal sanctions. Legal relationships that are fiduciary include trustee-trust beneficiary and guardian-ward. Maritain would agree that the representative-many relationship is similar to the trustee-trust beneficiary relationship. The fiduciary character of the relationship mandates that the trustee-representative act solely for the benefit of his trust beneficiaries, the many.

Because of the potential for abuse of the fiduciary relationship by representatives acting under the aegis of political parties, Maritain, in *Integral Humanism* as well as in *Scholasticism and Politics*, proposed a "recasting of political structures." to free those structures from the domination of political parties.[71] He thought that the British parliamentary system had outlived its usefulness; it "suited the age of liberalistic individualism." Under this recasting, "political life would involve . . . two distinct orders of functions": (1) the preparation and maturing of authoritative decisions; and (2) the actual making and implementation of those decisions. These two functions would be operative from the local political level to the national level:

> Thus we could conceive, at each level, an assembly invested with the first order of functions (preparation and deliberation), and an "executive" or *"praesidium"* invested with the second order of functions (decision and execution), composed of men who would not be elected by the given assembly, but *proposed* [Maritain's emphasis] by the organ of the superior order, and *accepted* [Maritain's emphasis] by the popular vote of the area which would be thus governed. (If somebody thus proposed is not accepted, another will be proposed, until acceptance by the people is reached.)[72]

The preparation and deliberation function would depend on representative assemblies and "of various social bodies: their duty would be to prepare the legislative and executive work in close collaboration with the governmental organs." Maritain wanted the representative assemblies to exercise "control and regulation" by, *inter alia*, controlling the budget and "the right to demand in certain determined conditions the revision of a law or the rejection of a man, the right of sovereign decisions in certain cases concerning in a major manner the life of a nation."[73] The second order of functions, the decisional and implementation functions, would precede from the top of the pyramid. These functions "would belong to governmental organs free from all preoccupations other than the common good, and for that very reason independent of the representative assemblies."[74] Independent from the first two functions only as to decisional and implementation.

The agenda or parameters of the governmental organs would have been established in the preparation and maturation stages by the many through their representatives. At the apex of the pyramid Maritain conceived of a "supreme organ" that emanated "itself from the multitude, but in an indirect way." Maritain wrote that "one could conceive" of the supreme organ being "designated and proposed by the representatives of the consultative assemblies and by the principal organs of the life of the country." This designation would be subject to the approval of the many through a popular referendum.[75]

The purpose of this "recasting" was to limit what Maritain perceived to be the pernicious influence of political parties on the democratic process:

> The governmental organs would thus be a second—indirect— expression of the political thought and of the concrete interests of human persons and social bodies. Independent of the representative assemblies, they would at the same time be independent of political parties. And these parties not being able to lay a hand on the State and on the advantages born from such a seizure, would themselves be saved from the principle of corruption which today renders them pernicious.[76]

Maritain's recasting was an attempt to ensure that a personalist and Christian-inspired democracy is based on politics from the ground up, from the many to the government, not vice versa. Subsidiarity was an important element of a democracy for Maritain, as noted earlier. In *Reflections on America* he commented favorably on the difference between European and America society—America was a country of "swarming multiplicity of particular communities." America, at least in the 1950s did not like the notion of state. "It feels more comfortable with the notion of *community* [Maritain's emphasis]."[77] Europe, on the other hand was "both atomized and so imbued with politics, so subjugated by political parties" that the movement from bourgeois liberal democracy to personalist democracy would require a long "and more exacting preparatory tilling of the soil."[78]

The recasting would place power at the local level where the many would have local access through their representatives to the preparation and development of government decisions. In effect, at the local level, Maritain's recasting would replace the committee system through which local government units do their preliminary work with consultative bodies elected by the many. These consulting bodies were not window dressing—they had genuine political power, i.e., the control of the purse. However, at the same time Maritain wanted to increase the political clout of the many.

Maritain advocated a large degree of autonomy for the many's representatives. The critical issue for representation in a democracy is: What is the scope of the representative's authority? Maritain followed Edmund Burke in holding that the representative is not expected to slavishly follow the dictates of his constituents. Burke said that the wishes of the constituents should "have great weight" with the representative and he is to "prefer their interest to his own." But the representative was not obligated to follow the wishes of his constituents when they are "contrary to the clearest conviction of his judgment and conscience."[79] Maritain agreed:

> They [representatives] are not mere instruments of a mythical general will; they are actual rulers of the people; they have to make their decisions conformably to the dictates of their conscience, to the laws of that specific branch of Ethics which is political Ethics, to the judgment of their virtue (if they have any) of political prudence, and to what they see required by the common good—even if by so doing they incur the displeasure of the people.[80]

Although the representative must follow the dictates of his conscience, he must also rule in communion with the people, which for Maritain meant that the representative must educate and awaken the people while governing them, which is different than "selling them ideas through sheer propaganda and advertising techniques."[81] Maritain then would reject modern television's ten-second "sound bite" as well as the other techniques of modern advertising which have permeated the politics of the Western democracies of the late twentieth century.

Maritain's position about the educational responsibilities of representatives is similar to Madison's, who expected the representative to "refine and enlarge the public views." The purpose of refining and enlarging was to filter the public views "through a medium of a chosen body of citizens" who would have a long-term perspective about what is best for the body politic. Madison's concern about "temporary or partial considerations," spur-of-the-moment decisions by the many, was shared by Maritain as noted above.[82] Maritain saw Machiavellianism resulting from hurried decisions that are not grounded on mature, careful evaluation of their long-term implications for the body politic.

How can Maritain's apparently divergent views on representation be reconciled? As pointed out earlier, Maritain's theory of democracy has similarities with the sentiments of the Antifederalists during the debate over the ratification of the United States Constitution. His theory of representation is another point of similarity. Maritain's recasting was his attempt to give full force and effect to the Antifederalists' theory of representation, as exemplified in the comments of George Mason, a leading Antifederalist theoretician, that "to make representation real and actual, the number of representatives ought to be adequate; they ought to mix with the people, think as they think, feel as they feel—ought to be perfectly amenable to them, and thoroughly acquainted with their interests and condition."[83]

By placing the preparation and deliberation function at the local level—the county, town or city level in the United States—Maritain provided for a large number of representatives and brought them closer to the people. His plan is also consistent with the autonomy that he was willing to allow representatives. A representative drawn from the local population, operating at the lowest level of government, personally known to his constituents, can be more persuasive in educating his constituents then a representative elected from a large geographical area. The local representative also has the trust and confidence of his neighbors to a greater extent than a representative not locally elected.

Also, the local representative would be more inclined to take seriously the fiduciary responsibilities that Maritain insisted was at the heart of the representative-citizen relationship. Maritain foresaw, because of the political problems of the French Third Republic, that parliamentary republicanism infected with unbridled individualism and controlled by political parties advocating their own special interests can have a debilitating effect on a democracy.[84] His recasting was designed to prevent the domination of the many by representatives with only ephemeral ties to the many. The recasting was not fully developed by Maritain. But its general theme underlies his belief in the people as the ultimate source of political power in a democracy.

SUMMARY

This study began with Maritain's thesis that there is an inexorable link between democracy and Christianity. A critical examination of that thesis has revealed that there is a warrant for his contention. On the theoretical level, Maritain's thesis is an outgrowth of his political ontology which emphasized the spiritual nature of human existence; a spiritual nature grounded in the Christian teaching of the brotherhood of man and moral freedom. Man's spiritual nature must be imbued with universality, must transcend self-interest, which is tied to man's immediate family or group, must be activated by the dynamic religion of Bergson. On the practical level, Maritain's thesis is persuasive in light of the empirical findings of Tocqueville concerning the nature of democracy. Those findings support Maritain's contention that democracy must be vivified by a spiritual force that can only be provided by religion—Christianity. Maritain's prescient observations that bourgeois liberal democracy with its empty head could not provide the western democracies with a moral charter that would combat the materialistic element endemic to democracy has been on target. The rise of atomization manifested in unbridled individualism and the excessive centralization of political power has come to pass just as Maritain foresaw.

Maritain was a true revolutionary. "Truth to tell there is nothing more scandalous and, in a sense, more revolutionary (for this is revolutionary even in regard to revolution) than the belief in a politics intrinsically Christian by its principles, its spirit, its modalities, and the claim to proceed in this world to a vitally Christian political action."[85] Maritain saw that Tocqueville had correctly analyzed the irresistible nature of democracy. In addition, Maritain also saw that the social gospel of Christianity was a natural and necessary accouterment for democracy. Necessary for a true democracy had to have a moral foundation to survive.

NOTES

1. See Raghavan Iyer, *The Moral and Political Thought of Mahatma Gandhi*, 2nd ed. (London: Concord Grove Press, 1983.), 37-87.

2. Thomas Merton, ed. *Gandhi on Non-Violence* (New York: New Directions Publishing Corp., 1964) 4. I do not suggest that the Christian social Gospel was the sole source of Gandhi's politics of purification. He relied primarily on the social teaching of his Hindu religion.

3. *Man and the State* 58-59.

4. *Integral Humanism*, 221.

5. See Mahatma Gandhi, *Non-Violence in Peace and War*, 2 vols. (Ahmedabad, India: Navajivan Publishing House, 1948), I, 170. No evidence has been discovered that suggests that Maritain and Gandhi ever communicated with each other. Maritain's and Gandhi's admirer, Thomas Merton, were friends. See John Howard Griffin and Yves R. Simon, *Jacques Maritain: Homage in Words and Pictures*, foreword by Anthony R. Simon (Albany, New York: Magi Books, 1974), 32-38. Merton, along with Maritain and Gandhi, believed that politics had to be purified with Christian morality. Maritain's integral humanism, in one form or another, was championed by Merton and Gandh

6. Defined by Maritain as the "power of truth," a definition that conforms to the meaning Gandhi gave the word.

7. *Man and the State*, 68-71.

8. Ibid.

9. Ibid.

10. Maritain described Alinsky as "a great friend of mine," who was "a courageous and admirably staunch organizer of 'people's communities' and an anti-racist leader whose methods are as effective as they are unorthodox." *The Peasant of the Garrone*, 23.

11. Sanford D. Horwitt, *Let Them Call Me Rebel: Saul Alinsky. His Life and Legacy* (New York: Alfred A. Knopf, 1989), 166. Maritain's support of Alinsky is an example of how Maritain saw his integral humanism working in a concrete historical situation.

12. See Jacques Maritain, "The End of Machiavellianism," *The Review of Politics*, vol. 4, no. 1 (January, 1942): 1.

13. Ibid.

14. *Integral Humanism*, 251. Gandhi accepted force in one situation; "He who cannot protect himself or his nearest and dearest or their honor by nonviolently facing death, may and ought to do so by violently dealing with the oppressor." *Non-Violence in Peace and War*, I, 77.

15. Neither Maritain or Bergson used the term "pardigmatic individual." The term has been appropriated by this study from A. S. Cua, *Dimensions of Moral Creativity: Paradigms, Principles, and Ideals* (University Park, Pennsylvania: Pennsylvania State University Press, 1978).

Cua's study traces the concept of what he calls paradigmatic individuals in Confucian thought. Cua's concept is applicable to Maritain's and Bergson's thought on moral leadership in a democracy. Cua says, at 37:

> In his manner of relating himself to a tradition, the paradigmatic
> individual in effect transfuses the content of his tradition into his
> own life. The effect is one of transfiguration. Herein lies the supreme
> venture—the risk of disapproval and condemnation of his fellow
> beings. This is perhaps the reason why the paradigmatic individuals
> can inspire devotion and enthusiasm and at the same time evoke
> hostility from their audience. Transfiguration can be achieved only
> after a struggle.

16. See *The Two Sources of Morality and Religion*, 227-237.

17. *Man and the State*, 139.

18. Ibid.

19. Ibid., 140.

20. Viereck and Maritain shared many political and social values. A comparison of their thought exceeds the scope of this study. Both were members and leaders of the Congress For Cultural Freedom, an anticommunist organization in the 1950s. Viereck served on the executive committee of the Congress's American Committee. Viereck mentions Maritain as a member of the Congress with, *inter alia*, Benedetto Croce and John Dewey. Peter Viereck, *Shame and Glory of the Intellectuals* (Boston: Beacon Press, 1953), 176. Viereck also praised Maritain for his public opposition to the Pope's support of Franco's regime in Spain. Ibid., 229.

21. Peter Viereck, *The Unadjusted Man: A New Hero For Americans* (New York: Capricorn Books, 1962), 5.

22. Ibid.

23. Ibid., 141.

24. Ibid.

25. John M. Dunaway, ed., *Exiles and Fugitives: The Letters of Jacques and Raissa Maritain, Allen Tate, and Caroline Gordon* (Baton Rouge, Louisiana: Louisiana State University Press, 1992) Letter No. 29, p. 40.

26. Ibid. Appendix A, Letter of Jacques Maritain to Frederick Morgan, February 25, 1952, p. 99.

27. See Fred Halstead, *Out Now: A Participant's Account of the American Movement Against the War* (New York: Monad Press, 1978), 77; Myra MacPherson, *Long Time Passing:Vietnam and the Haunted Generation* (New York: New American Library, 1984) 112-114, 391-471. MacPherson mentions that the Rev. Timothy Healy, S.J., former president of Georgetown University was opposed to the war on religious grounds.

At the time Father Healy was a professor at the City University of New York.

28. *Man and the State*, 146.

29. Ibid., 54.

30. Ibid.

31. Ibid.

32. Ibid., 55.

33. Mohandas Gandhi, *Hind Swaraj* (Navajivan: 1938) in *The Moral and Political Thought of Mahatama Gandhi*, 363. Iyer points out that Kautilya was an Indian political theorist who like Machiavelli separated politics from morality. Ibid., 365.

34. *Scholasticism and Politics*, 22.

35. *The Range of Reason*, 134, *et seq.*

36. Ibid., 134ff. Maritain's contention that *The Prince* did not plow new ground is supported by Allan H. Gilbert, *Machiavelli's Prince and its Forerunners: The Prince as a Typical Book de Regimine Principum* (Durham, North. Carolina.: Duke University Press, 1938), a book that Maritain thought was "the best historical commentary on Machiavelli." *Range of Reason*, 134.

Maritain thought that Gilbert was correct in regarding *The Prince* as a typical genre of the time. Yet, *The Prince* was the culmination of the genre, "not only because of changes in society, but because its inspiration utterly reverses and corrupts the medieval notion of government. It is a typical book . . ., but which typically puts the series of these books to death." Ibid. (unnumbered footnote).

37. Ibid., 135.

38. Ibid.

39. Ibid., 137.

40. Ibid., 141.

41. Ibid.

42. Ibid., 137. Maritain cited Matth. 23, 3.

43. Ibid., 154.

44. Herman Rauschning, *m'a dit* (*The Voice of Destruction*), 1940, as cited by Maritain, *Range of Reason*, 144.

45. Ibid.

46. Ibid., 142.

47. *Range of Reason*, 143.

48. Ibid., 143-144.

49. Ibid., 144.

50. Ibid.

51. Ibid., 145.

52. Ibid.

53. Ibid., 146-147.

54. Ibid., 138.

55. *Man and the State*, 62-63.

56. Ibid., 155.

57. Ibid. See Friedrich Meinecke, *The German Catastrophe: Reflections and Recollections*, trans. Sidney B. Fay (Boston: Beacon Press, 1963).

58. Ibid., 148.

59. *Integral Humanism*, 260.

60. *Man and the State*, 59.

61. *The Range of Reason*, 165.

62. Ibid.

63. Ibid., 63.

64. Ibid., 153.

65. Henri Bergson, *An Introduction to Metaphysics*, trans. T. E. Hulme, translation approved by Bergson, intro. Thomas A. Goudge (New York: Macmillan Publishing Co., 1955), 40.

66. *The Range of Reason.*, 156.

67. Ibid.

68. *Man and the State*, 130.

69. Ibid., 134.

70. *The Random House Dictionary of the English Language*, 2nd ed., s.v. "fiduciary."

71. *Scholasticism and Politics*, 114. *Intergral Humanism*, 175.

72. *Scholasticism and Politics*, 115.

73. Ibid.

74. Ibid.

75. Ibid., 116.

76. Ibid.

77. *Reflections on America*, 162-163.

78. Ibid.

79. *Speeches at Mr. Burke's Arrival at Bristol, and at the Conclusion of the Poll*, 1774, in *The Works of the Right Honorable Edmund Burke*, 8 vols. (London, 1855-64), I, 446-447.

80. *Man and the State*, 136.

81. Ibid., 137.

82. *The Federalist Papers*, no. 10 (J. Madison).

83. Jonathan Elliott, *The Debates in the State Conventions on the Adoption of the Federal Constitution as Recommended by the General Convention at Philadelphia*, in 1787, 2nd ed., 5 vols. (Philadelphia: J. B.

Lippincott, 1896), III, 32.

84.   Tony Judt, "'We have Discovered History': Defeat, Resistance, and the Intellectuals in France," *The Journal of Modern History*, vol. 64, Supplement (December, 1992): S147.

According to Judt, for the general population and especially for French intellectuals, "The Third Republic, it is said, died unloved. Few sought seriously to defend it in July, 1940, and it passed away unmourned." The apathy over the Republic's demise was due to its bourgeois liberal character. Judt quotes Mounier that ". . . the whole rotten edifice will have to crumble." Another commentator likened the Third Republic to an insurance company, while a third commentator remarked that "The only way to love France today is to hate it in its present form." Ibid., S148-S149.

85.   *Integral Humanism*, 265.

CHAPTER 8

CRITIQUE OF MARITAIN'S DEMOCRACY

Maritain's idea of a Christian-inspired democracy is open to the criticism that his conception of democracy is utopian. The probability of such a society and culture as Maritain envisioned ever being actualized in the modern world of the large nation-state is the same as the probability of the actualization of a social order led by the philosopher-king of Plato. Such a society never was and never will be. Conflict is indigenous to modern societies, particularly to modern western democracies. From the birth of Christ to the present-day human beings have shown a marked propensity to resolve conflict by force or self-interest rather than by turning the other cheek or by making one's neighbor's welfare equal with one's own.

This type of criticism is fueled by the failures of the so-called Christian Democratic parties in Western Europe and Latin America—parties created after World War II at least partially on the basis of Maritain's political philosophy. Maritain admitted that these parties had failed to establish an authentically Christian-inspired political order. He criticized the so-called Christian Democrats:

> I had in mind a politics which, while drawing its inspiration from the Christian spirit and Christian principles, would involve only the initiative and responsibilities of the citizens who conduct it, without being in the slightest degree a politics dictated by the Church, or committing her to responsibility. May I add that until today—and despite (or because of) the entry on the scene, in different countries, of political parties labeled "Christian" (most of which are primarily combinations of electoral interests)—the hope for the advent of a *Christian politics* (corresponding in the practical order to what a *Christian philosophy* is in the speculative order) has been completely frustrated. [Maritain's emphases][1]

Maritain continued that he knew of "only one example of an authentic 'christian revolution,' and that is what President Eduardo Frei is attempting at this very moment in Chile, and it is not sure that he will succeed."[2]

Maritain observed that the primary failing of the Christian Democrats was that they had not developed an authentic Christian political philosophy. They had failed to implement the social gospel. Too often the Christian Democrats had aligned themselves with the Left. A true Christian political philosophy is not left or right—"In reality, however it [Christian political philosophy] would have absolutely original positions proceeding, from very different principles than the conceptions of the world, life, the family, and the city, which prevail in the various parties of the left."[3]

Maritain criticized the Left and the Right:

> The pure man of the left detests being, always preferring in principle, in the words of Rousseau *what is not* to *what is*. The pure man of the right detests justice and charity, always preferring in principle, in the words of Goethe ". . . *injustice* to *disorder*." Nietzsche is a noble and beautiful example of the man of the right, and Tolstoy, of the man of the left [Maritain's emphases].

The missing link in the so-called Christian Democratic parties' failure is that the ground for an authentic Christian politics had not been prepared through a lengthy process of education. It cannot be emphasized strongly enough that Maritain's type of democracy is dependent on an educational system that inculcates the spiritual nature of man into the youth of his city. Without this educational foundation any attempt to ground a social order on man's spiritual nature, which is the ground for the social gospel, is doomed to fail.

Maritain did not deny the existence of conflict. In his personalist or Christian-inspired democracy the major tactic for the resolution of conflict would be the nonviolent technique of *satyagraha* developed in India by Mahatma Gandhi, a system of conflict resolution with strong ties to Christ's teaching, as noted above. Another element in the resolution of conflict would be the prophetic shock minority also discussed above. They would sharpen the issues involved in the conflict and provide the moral leadership to propose innovative moral solutions to problems.

Lastly, there can be little doubt that Maritain believed that friendship infused with Christian charity could at least soften the harshness and inflexibility endemic to conflict by creating a sense of good will and concord within the democracy that would inhibit unbridled self-interest. If such a belief is unrealistic, then Maritain's idea of democracy was utopian. However, the failure of the Christian Democrats in Europe should not be an indictment of Maritain's thinking on democracy. Their failure to implement the social teaching of the gospel while aligning themselves too often with the doctrinaire Left was in opposition to critical elements in

Maritain's thinking about democracy.

THE TIME FOR MARITAIN'S DEMOCRACY

Maritain knew that it would take a long time to prepare a culture for a Christian-inspired democracy. Writing in the late 1950s Maritain did not see the millennium on the horizon. In *Man and the State*, he was clear that the prospects for a Christian-inspired democracy are long-term. He also realized that there would be no return to the Middle Ages when the Catholic Church, armed with temporal authority, dominated from above. He saw the Christian-inspired democracy rising from the ashes of bourgeois liberal democracy. As the forces of materiality overwhelmed being as personality, Maritain foresaw a counter reaction of an invigorated spirituality developing from what he called a new Christendom. The New Christendom would vivify a political order from below, from the many. Only through a "new Christendom, one that is yet to come that [the] ethical and affective value of the word 'democracy' answering to what we may call popular civic consciousness, could really be saved."[4]

Maritain believed that while Christianity's social and political ideals and values had been given a full theoretical exposition, they had never been fully developed in the practical everyday world. As a result, "As regards the effective realization or refraction of the Gospel in the socio-temporal sphere, we are still truly in a prehistoric age."[5] The New Christendom would identify with the many and would emphasize the practical application of the social gospel. In turn the political order would vivify the New Christendom by providing an environment for its implementation of the social gospel. The New Christendom would not derive its potency as a political force from its temporal political power. It would be through ordinary Christians who comprise a substantial part of the many that the movement to the personalist and Christian-inspired democracies would actualize the social gospel:

> Thus the superior dignity and authority of the Church asserts itself, not
> by virtue of a coercion exercised on the civil power, but by virtue of
> the spiritual enlightenment conveyed to the souls of the citizens, who
> must freely bear judgment, according to their own personal conscience,
> on every matter pertaining to the political common good.[6]

The argument that Maritain's democracy is utopian has been vitiated by recent empirical evidence that supports his contention that a personalist or Christian-inspired democracy is a practical possibility. From 1979 to 1984, a group of social scientists, led by sociologist Robert Bellah, conducted an extensive study of American society.[7] A detailed examination of the group's findings is beyond the scope of this study. In a nutshell, the group found general dissatisfaction with the rampant individualism and unbridled self-interest that dominates late twentieth-century American society. "Many Americans are concerned to find meaning in life not primarily through self-cultivation but through intense relations with others."

Bellah and his associates found that a large segment of Americans are trying to reintegrate public and private life. The social scientists called this "reappropriating tradition." The people who are involved in this process "are drawing on our republican and biblical traditions, trying to make what has become second languages into our first language again."[8] Among Bellah's group's conclusions is the belief, slowly becoming widespread, that the problems of America are primarily "moral and have to do with the meaning of life." They suggest that "Perhaps enduring commitment to those we love and civic friendship toward our fellow citizens are preferable to restless competition and anxious self-love."[9]

Needless to say Maritain would agree with the social scientists. He would remind them that Tocqueville's observations about the destructiveness of individualism and materiality on a democratic society have been proven correct. And he would tell them that the only way to counter the atomization of a democracy is through the social gospel of Christianity. Maritain would also see in the empirical findings of Bellah's group the beginning of a process described by Bergson in *The Two Sources*. For Bergson, the open morality is slowly developed through a deep-seated emotion that lies at the heart of the human psyche. As the creative force of this emotion is released, and Bergson considered Christian charity to be part of this creative emotional force, a "social conscience" starts to exert its influence. The creative emotion of the open morality of Christianity combines with the closed morality of an established social order to create the social conscience that Maritain thought so necessary for a true democratic social order. Bergson described this commingling process. "Once again, there is some difficulty in comparing the two moralities because they are no longer to be found in a pure state. The first [closed] has handed on to the second [open] something of its compulsive force; the second has diffused over the other something of its perfume."[10]

MARITAIN'S UTOPIANISM

Another example of Maritain's alleged utopianism is his writings on world government. Just as a society has never emerged based on the Christian social gospel so also has the movement toward a world government not only never materialized, but the opposite tendency has taken place—a movement toward the proliferation of nation-states with built-in antagonisms grounded on ethnic, racial, or religious antagonisms.

Maritain was quick to point out that his views on world government were those of a political theoretician "and not from that of practical activity."[11] He believed that a world government was a necessity given the tremendous destructive force of nuclear weapons combined with the amorality of the nation-states' conduct of foreign affairs. "But as concerns the *external or foreign* [Maritain's emphasis] activity of the State, that is, its relations with other States, there is nothing to check the trend of modern States . . . toward supreme domination and supreme amorality, nothing except the opposite force of the other States."[12]

Maritain foresaw the ineffectiveness of the United Nations in putting a stop to unbridled rapaciousness in international relations.[13] He also recognized that the idea of a world government is "fine and beautiful, but utterly impossible of realization, and therefore most dangerous, for it runs the risk of diverting toward a brilliant utopia efforts which should be directed toward more humble but possible achievements."[14] If the idea were merely "a beautiful idea" he would not "care much for it." He thought that it was a "sound" and "great" idea.[15]

The only way that a world government could become a practical reality was through what Maritain called a "fully political theory of world organization."[16] The peoples of the world would retain their various nation-states. But, they would unite in recognizing and pursuing a common good. The "essential part" in the creation of the world government would be:

> played by the will of the people, in every nation, to live together, in the world. I mean a will so powerful as to sweep away the obstacles caused by the myth of the States as sovereign persons or by the bias of governments, and the obstacles, still greater, caused in the people themselves by misfortune and fatigue, slowness of reason, and natural self-interest.[17]

Maritain's "world government" was not a "government" in the sense of an all-powerful Superstate plenary to the individual nation-states. "The quest of such a Superstate capping the Nations is nothing else, in fact, than the quest of the old utopia of a universal empire."[18] Instead, for Maritain "world government" meant the voluntary coming together of the peoples of the world to form a community of interests. He emphasized that the coming together must be voluntary and it must rise from the ground up, from the peoples, not from the government entities. His concept of world government is consistent with his theory of democracy in that both are grounded on the cultural and social hegemony of the people. Maritain's democracy and his concept of world government evidence his distrust of large government. As noted above, decentralization was a key element in his personalist democracy.

Maritain saw the development of a common good arising from "suffering together. When men form a political society, they do not want to share in common suffering out of love for each other. They want to accept common suffering out of love for the common task and the common good." The common suffering will be felt most in the Western democracies:

> The very existence of a world wide society will also inevitably imply a certain—relative no doubt, yet quite serious and appreciable—equalization of the standards of life of all individuals. Let us put it in crude terms: perhaps, if the issue were made sufficiently clear to them, people in Occidental nations would be ready to accept, for the sake of peace and of a world political organization ensuring lasting peace, a serious lowering of their standards of life in order to provide people on the other side of the iron curtain with an equivalent raising of their standards of life. Yet this would suppose a kind of moral heroism, for which, I deem, we are badly prepared. —People are unhappy, and it will be necessary for them to confront new obligations and sacrifices connected with the life of other men at the other end of the world, in order to promote in the long run peace, happiness, and freedom for all.[19]

Just as in his theory of democracy Maritain looked to the Christian doctrines of the brotherhood of man and the inherent equality of each person before God to be the spearhead of the movement toward a world government as he understood that term. Maritain recognized that man will "never be the *Master and Possessor* [Maritain's emphasis] of nature and history; it is a lie to try and convince him of such a thing." The Christian must "*intervene* in the destiny of the world, winning at great pains and at the risk of a thousand dangers—through science and political action—a power over nature and over history."[20]

Maritain conceded that the formation of a world government—like the development of a Christian-inspired democracy—would take a long time. He thought it "regrettable" that almost 2000 years after "the good tidings of Bethlehem, mankind is still in a prehistoric age with regard to the application of the Gospel in actual life."[21] Just as a particular society must be prepared through education for a Christian-inspired democracy, so also must there be political preparation for the world government. To that end Maritain proposed the creation of a "Supra-National Advisory Council," which "would be deprived of any *power* whatsoever, but endowed with unquestionable *moral authority* [Maritain's emphases]." The advisory council would be composed of "the highest and most experienced authorities in moral and juridical sciences" from all of the nations. The members would be elected by the peoples of the world from lists of qualified candidates proposed by the "highest institutions and governments" of each state. Members would become citizens of the world. They would have no power. "No government could appeal to them to make any decisions, they would have no juridical connection with the United Nations, they would be simply free to tell the governments and the nations what they held to be just."[22]

Again Maritain's thinking about world government mirrors his theory of democracy. The advisory council would be a group of the paradigmatic individuals that Maritain, and Bergson, saw as essential to the proper functioning of a democracy. The advisory council would have the same function as the paradigmatic individual in a democracy—to mold public opinion. Maritain saw that an "organized" international public opinion was "something indispensable" to the formation of a common good.[23]

Some conclusions can be drawn about Maritain's alleged utopianism. The evidence is persuasive that he was not a sentimental humanitarian in the sense that Irving Babbitt wrote about. Sentimental humanitarianism is a hallmark of Rousseauistic thinking. Anything associated with Rousseau would be per se antithetical to Maritain. His concept of fellowship and concord were not philosophically grounded on compassion or pity, as noted above, but on the teachings of Jesus Christ. Quite simply Maritain believed that those who profess Christianity should live—as part of the action and reaction that is indigenous to a political order—the Christian social gospel, just as he did in his personal life.

The evidence is less convincing that his views about world government were not tinged with utopianism. Here there is no empirical evidence in the form of a study similar to Bellah's group that would support the recognition of the peoples of the world that they have a community of interests. Although Maritain's observations about the economic interdependence of the world have proven correct, he conceded that economic interdependence was not enough.[24] It [economic interdependence] can "but impose by material necessity a partial and fragmentary, growing bit by bit, political interdependence which is reluctantly and hatefully accepted," that "runs against the grain of nature" as long as nations have or believe they have full political autonomy.[25]

NONBELIEVERS AND DEMOCRACY

Maritain's Christian-inspired democracy can be viewed as utopian precisely because it is Christian inspired. What about the nonbelievers, the atheists and the non-Christians? Is it practical to expect countries like Japan, India, and Indonesia with their traditions of Buddhism, Islam, and Eastern religions to eventually adopt a political order grounded on the Christian social gospel? Maritain never addressed this issue. A sense of his thinking can be extrapolated from his writings and it would only be a sense, an educated guess. Maritain was concerned with Western civilization. His Christian-inspired democracy was conceived as the best type of political and social order—the best kind of culture—for the Western European nations and the United States. Maritain certainly would not recommend to anyone the perverted Western bourgeois liberal type of democracy with its anything goes philosophy that is endemic to Western civilization in the late twentieth century.

His expansive definition of democracy as a way of life or state of mind that emphasizes the spiritual nature of man is broad enough to encompass any culture that embraces man's spirituality with political institutions that provide for universal suffrage and rule ultimately by the people. Certainly the Buddhist and Islamic cultures have the requisite spiritual underpinning that Maritain saw as critical for the best type of democracy. If a Buddhist or Islamic culture developed with a Buddhist or Islamic moral charter and incorporated the democratic principles of the Christian-inspired or personalist democracy with Buddhist or Islamic modifications similar, for example, to the adoption by the United States at the time of the American Revolution of the common law of England as modified by the unique American experience, then he would probably regard such a regime as one that indirectly had been influenced by Christianity and to that extent was Christian inspired.

Maritain was also aware of a basic common substratum of moral and ethical principles subsumed within all of the world's great religions. Many scholars of comparative religion have cataloged these similarities.[26] For example the Christian teaching of the forgiveness of enemies is echoed in Judaism: "The most beautiful thing a man can do is to forgive wrong;" and Islam: "Forgive thy servants seventy times a day;" also Buddhism: "Never is hate diminished by hatred; It is only diminished by love—This is an eternal law."[27]

Maritain saw the mystics of all religions as a unifying force because their mysticism springs from the same source:

> All authentic mysticism which has developed in non-Christian countries, should be regarded as a fruit of the same supernatural life, that supernatural life which Christ, sovereignly generous in his gifts, communicates to those souls of good will who do not visibly belong to his flock.[28]

Maritain believed that the theological differences inherent in the world's religions do not constitute an insurmountable barrier to cooperation between the religions and the adoption in some form of Christian principles as applied to the political order by the non-Christian faiths. Maritain's position has been partly vindicated as regards Islam. Pope John Paul II has emphasized the "high regard" that the Catholic Church has for Muslims. John Paul continued that "As a result of their monotheism, believers in Allah are particularly close to us."[29] Given the commonality of a core of religious and ethical beliefs, I think that it is safe to say that the basic principles of Maritain's Christian-inspired democracy have a potential universal appeal to all nations and cultures.

CHRISTIANITY AND DEMOCRACY CRITICIZED

A better-reasoned and more sophisticated critique of Maritain's conception of democracy than its utopianism is the criticism that attacks Maritain's basic thesis that democracy and Christianity have a symbiotic relationship. According to this perspective, not only do Christianity and democracy not have a symbiotic relationship, they are antithetical. This was the ground for Erik R. von Kuehnelt-Leddihn's, "A Critique of Democracy," an attack not aimed specifically at Maritain or at the alleged nexus between Christianity and democracy.[30] Distilled to its essence, in the part relevant to this discussion, Kuehnelt-Leddihn's argument is that democracy is inherently relativistic because all voices must be heard on a particular issue with eventually the lowest common denominator prevailing. To illustrate his point, Kuehnelt-Leddihn hypothesized an election in which the candidates are a "True Christian," a "Bad Pagan," and a "Good Pagan." "The True Christian as a candidate in a thoroughly democratic society is almost unthinkable" because the Christian's conscience will not let his absolute values be corrupted by the relativism that is demanded in finding the lowest common denominator.

Kuehnelt-Leddihn explains:

> The Christian politician would be sincere, frank, serious. He would confess ignorance where need be, he would oppose his constituents when his conscience advocates disagreement, he would refuse to distort facts by "popularizing" them thus flattering the intellectual vanity of the credulous masses The Bad Pagan simply lies to his voters. He either is determined not to stick to his promises or to act against his conscience. The Good Pagan is in the worst situation; he lies quite subconsciously, to himself. He believes, probably in all sincerity, that one can square the circle, that one's own conscience, absolute truth, the feasible and permissible, ethical and practical, public opinion and the useful can all be brought under the same denominator.[31]

In Kuehnelt-Leddihn's words "the inferior human currency drives the better one out of circulation. The Good Christian's position is an almost hopeless one."[32] Although in July, 1946, when Kuehnelt-Leddihn was writing he could comment that ". . . the *limited* [emphasis in original] material rewards a political career should offer thus providing the democrat with no economic advantages and incentives for reelection," would provide a bulwark against unbridled self-interest in the politician, such is not the case in the late twentieth-century American democracy where the rapaciousness of the political class is seemingly uncontrollable.

Maritain would probably argue that Kuehnelt-Leddihn's criticism is valid for the empty-headed bourgeois liberal democracy, which Maritain considered the summit of a relativistic political order with its lowest common denominator culture. Kuehnelt-Leddihn's criticism, however, is consistent with Maritain's conception of democracy. Democracy must have a moral charter that acts as a prophylactic force on self-interest and unbridled individualism, a moral charter that fights relativism by trumpeting a core set of moral values that are generally accepted by a majority of citizens. That moral force must transcend the culture. In Western civilization and culture, the historical force that in the past has provided a restraining influence has been Christianity.

Christopher Dawson, a Catholic thinker with ideas similar to Maritain and a thinker who like Maritain and others foresaw the suicidal destructiveness of a political order that forgets its religious heritage, made a comprehensive study of Christianity's effect on Western culture and the effect of religion on culture in general. Dawson's erudition and scholarship were praised by Christian and non-Christian thinkers. His research and historical analysis supports Maritain's ideas about democracy. Dawson summed up his findings:

> We are only just beginning to understand how intimately and profoundly the vitality of a society is bound up with its religion. It is the religious impulse which supplies the cohesive force which unifies a society and a culture. The great civilizations of the world do not produce the great religions as a kind of cultural by-product; in a very real sense, the great religions are the foundations on which the great civilizations rest. A society which has lost its religion becomes sooner or later a society which has lost its culture.
>
> What then is to be the fate of this great modern civilization of ours? A civilization which has gained an extension and a wealth of power and knowledge which the world has never known before. Is it to waste its forces in the pursuit of selfish and mutually destructive aims, and to perish for lack of vision? Or can we hope that society will once again be animated by a common faith and hope, which will have the power to order our material and intellectual achievements in an enduring spiritual unity.[33]

The study ends where it began—with being. It is being imbued with true caring, with a generosity of spirit that is necessary for a democracy to avoid the excessive levelization fueled by materialism and unbridled individualism that is part of the warp and woof of a bourgeois liberal democratic polity. That generosity of spirit can be found in its fullest expression in Christianity.

NOTES

1. *The Peasant of the Garonne*, 22-23.
2. *The Peasant of the Garonne*, 23.
3. Ibid., citing Maritain's *Lettre sur l'Indépendance* (Paris: Desclée De Brouwer, 1935), 42-43.
4. *Integral Humanism*, 202.
5. Ibid., 243.
6. *Man and the State*, 164.
7. Robert Bellah, et al., *Habits of the Heart: Individualism and*

Commitment in American Life (Berkeley: University of California Press, 1985).

8. *Habits of the Heart*, 291-292.

9. Ibid., 295.

10. *The Two Sources of Morality and Religion*, 49-51.

11. *Man and the State*, 188.

12. Ibid., 193.

13. Ibid.

14. Ibid., 200.

15. Ibid., 200-201.

16. Ibid., 202.

17. Ibid., 210.

18. *Man and the State*, 204.

19. Ibid., 207-208.

20. *The Peasant of the Garonne*, 201.

21. *Man and the State*, 212.

22. Ibid., 212-214.

23. *Man and the State*, 215.

24. Ibid., 190-191.

25. Ibid.

26. See, for exanple C. S. Lewis, *The Abolition of Man* (New York: Macmillan Publishing Company, 1947); S. Radhakrishnan, *Eastern Religions and Western Thought*, 2d ed. (London: Oxford University Press, 1940); Jeffrey Moses, *Oneness: Great Principles Shared by all Religions*, intro. Mother Teresa (New York: Fawcett Columbine, 1989).

27. *Oneness*, 72-73.

28. *Eastern Religions and Western Thought*, 321, quoting Maritain from *Decgrees of Knowledge*, 1937 edition of the English translation, 357. Also, Ibid.:

> Because there is a flock the Shepherd who leads it is also the guide of those "other sheep" who, without knowing him, have also received of his plenitude and who have not yet heard his voice. . . The saints who belong to the invisible Church enable us to recognize their far-off brothers who are ignorant of her and who belong to her invisibly.

29. John Paul II, *Crossing the Threshold of Hope* (New York: Alfred A. Knopf, 1994) 91. In a preceding chapter, the Pope criticized Buddhism. Ibid., 84-90.

30. Erik K. von Kuehnelt-Leddihn, "A Critique of Democracy," *The New Scholasticism*, vol. XX, no. 3, July, 1946 at 195.

31. "A Critique of Democracy," 219-221.

32. Ibid.

33. Christopher Dawson, *Dynamics of World History*, ed. by John J. Mulloy (New York: Sheed and Ward, 1956) 129. See also, *inter alia*, Dawson's, *The Making of Europe: An Introduction into the History of European Unity* and *Religion and the Rise of Western Culture*.

SELECTED BIBLIOGRAPHY

PRIMARY SOURCES

BOOKS BY JACQUES MARITAIN

Maritain, Jacques. *A Preface To Metaphysics*. New York: Sheed and Ward, 1942.

———. *An Essay on Christian Philosophy*. Trans. by Edward H. Flannery. New York: Philosophical Library, 1955.

———. *An Introduction to the Basic Problems of Moral Philosophy*. Translated by Cornelia Borgerhoff. Albany, New York: Magi Books, 1990.

———. *An Introduction to Philosophy*. Translated by E. I. Watkins. New York: Sheed and Ward, 1930

———. *AntiSemitism*. London: Geoffrey Bless: The Centenary Press, 1939.

———. *Art and Scholasticism with Other Essays*. Translated by J. F. Scanlan. New York: Charles Scribner's Sons, 1930.

———. *Christianity and Democracy*. Translated by Doris C. Anson. San Francisco: Ignatius Press, 1986. Originally published, 1943.

———. *Creative Intuition in Art and Poetry*. New York: Pantheon, 1953.

———. *Education at the Crossroads*. New Haven: Yale University Press, 1943.

———. *Existence and the Existent*. English version by Lewis Galantiere and Gerald B. Phelan. Lanham, Maryland: University Press of America, 1987. Originally published in 1947.

———. *God and the Permission of Evil*. Translated by Joseph W. Evans. Milwaukee, Wisconsin: Bruce Publishing Co., 1966.

———. *Integral Humanism*. New translation by Joseph W. Evans. New York: Charles Scribner's Sons, 1968. Originally published in 1936.

———. *Man and the State*. Chicago: University of Chicago Press, 1951.

———. *Notebooks*. Translated by Joseph Evans. Albany, New York: Magi

Books, 1984. Originally published in 1964.

―――. *On The Grace and Humanity of Jesus*. Translated by Joseph Evans. New York: Herder and Herder, 1969.

―――. *On The Philosophy of History*. Edited by Joseph W. Evans. Clifton, New Jersey: Augustus M. Kelley, 1973. Originally published in 1957.

―――. *The Peasant of the Garonne*. Translated by Michael Cuddihy and Elizabeth Hughes. New York: Holt, Rinehart and Winston, 1968.

―――. *The Person and the Common Good*. Translated by John J. FitzGerald. Notre Dame, Indiana: Notre Dame University Press, 1968. Originally published in 1947.

―――. *The Range of Reason*. New York: Charles Scribner's Sons, 1942.

―――. *Ransoming The Time*. Translated by Henry L. Binsse. New York: Charles Scribner's Sons, 1941.

―――. *Reflections On America*. New York: Charles Scribner's Sons, 1958.

―――. *The Responsibility of the Artist*. New York: n.p., 1960.

―――. *The Rights of Man and Natural Law*. London: Geoffrey Bless, The Centenary Press, 1944.

―――. *Scholasticism and Politics*. Edited translation by Mortimer J. Adler. London: Geoffrey Bless, 1940.

―――. *Theonas*. Translated by F. J. Sheed. New York: Sheed and Ward, 1933.

―――. *The Things That Are Not Caesar's*. Translated by J. F. Scanlan. New York: Charles Scribner's Sons, 1931.

―――. *Three Reformers*. London: Sheed and Ward, 1950.

―――. *Truth and Human Fellowship*. Princeton, New Jersey: Princeton University Press, 1957.

―――. *The Twilight of Civilization*. Translated by Lionel Landry. New York: Sheed and Ward, 1944.

Maritain, Jacques, Peter Wust, and Christopher Dawson. *Essays in Order*. New York: The MacMillan Company, 1931.

ARTICLES BY JACQUES MARITAIN

Maritain, Jacques. "The End of Machiavellianism." *The Review of Politics*. Vol. 4. No. 1. January, 1942.

―――. "Poetic Experience." *The Review of Politics*. Vol. 6. No. 4. October, 1944.

————. "Right and Left." *Blackfriars*. Vol. XVIII. No. 212. November, 1937.

————. "Society Without Money." *The Review of Social Economy* 43, 1985, p. 73.

————. "The Conflict of Methods at the End of the Middle Ages." *The Thomist*. Vol. III. No. 4. October, 1941.

———— and Raïssa Maritain. "Living and Contemplation." *Spiritual Life*. Vol. 5. No. 2. June, 1959.

————. "The Immortality of Man." *The Review of Politics*. Vol. 3. No. 4. October, 1941.

OTHER PRIMARY SOURCES

Alinsky, Saul. *Reveille for Radicals*. Chicago: University of Chicago Press, 1946.

Anderson v. Celebreeze, 460 U.S. 780 (1983).

Aristotle. *Politics*. Translated by Benjamin Jowett. New York: Carlton House, n.d.

————. *De Anima*. Translated, commentaries and glossary by Hippocrates G. Apostle. Grinnell, Iowa: The Peripatetic Press, 1981.

————. *The Nichomachean Ethics*. Loeb Classical Library. Translated by H. Rackham. Cambridge: Harvard University Press, 1934.

Augustine, Saint. *City of God*. Translated by Henry Bettenson. Introduction by John O'Meara. New York: Penguin Books, 1982.

Bellah, Robert, et al., *Habits of the Heart: Individualism and Commitment in American Life*. Berkeley: University of California Press, 1985.

Berdiaeff, Nicolas. *The Beginning and the End*. Translated by R. M. French. New York: Harper and Brothers, 1953.

Bergson, Henri. *The Two Sources of Morality and Religion*. Translated by R. Ashley Auda, Cloudesly Brereton, and W. Horsfall Carter. Notre Dame, Indiana: University of Notre Dame Press, 1977.

————. *Creative Evolution*. Translated by Arthur Mitchell. Lanham, Maryland: University Press of America, 1983.

————. *Essay on the Immediate Data of Consciousness*. London: Allen and Unwin, 1910. Translated into English as *Time and Free Will*.

————. *The Creative Mind*. Translated by Mabelle L. Andison. New York: The Philosophical Library, 1946.

————. *An Introduction to Metaphysics*. Approved translation by T. E. Hulme. New York: Macmillan Publishing Co., 1955.

Bernanos, George. *Plea for Liberty.* Translated by Henry Lorin Binsee. New York: Pantheon Books, Inc., 1944.

Bloy, Leon. *Pilgrim of the Absolute.* Selected by Räissa Maritain. Translated by John Coleman and Henry Lorin Binsse. New York: Pantheon Books, 1947.

Brandeis, Louis D. and Samuel Warren. "The Right To Privacy." 4 *Harvard Law Review* 193 (1890).

Burke, Edmund. *Reflections on the Revolution in France.* Buffalo, New York: Prometheus Books, 1987.

————. *The Works of the Right Honorable Edmund Burke.* 12 vols. Eighth Edition. Boston: Little Brown and Company, 1884.

Chernyshevsky, Nicolai. *What Is To Be Done?* Translated by Michael Katz. Annotated by William G. Wagner. Ithaca, New York: Cornell University Press, 1989.

Cua, Antonio. *Dimensions of Moral Creativity: Paradigms, Principles and Ideas.* University Park, Pennsylvania: Pennsylvania State University Press, 1978.

Dawson, Christopher. *The Making of Europe: An Introduction to the History of European Unity.* New York: Barnes & Noble, 1994. Originally published in 1932.

————. *Chrisianity in East and West.* LaSalle, Illinois: Sherwood Sugden & Company, 1981.

————. *Religion and the Rise of Western Culture.* New York: Doubleday, 1957.

————. *Dynamics of World History.* New York: Sheed and Ward, 1956.

————. *The Historical Reality of Christian Culture.* New York: Harper & Brothers, 1960.

————. *The Movement of World Revolution.* New York: Sheed and Ward, 1959.

Dostoevsky, Fyodor. *The Brothers Karamazov.* Translated by Constance Garrett, revised by Ralph Matlaw. New York: W. W. Norton & Co., 1976.

————. *The Devils.* Translated and Introduction by David Magarshack. New York: Penguin Books, 1953.

————. *The Diary of a Writer.* Translated and annotated by Boris Brasol. Introduction by Joseph Frank. Salt Lake City: Peregrine Smith Books, 1985.

————. *Notes From Underground.* Translated and introduction by Jessie Coulson. New York: Penguin Books, 1972.

Elliot, Jonathan. *The Debates in the Several State Conventions on the Adoption of the Federal Constitution as Recommended by the General*

Convention at Philadelphia in 1787.   Philadelphia: J. B. Lippincott, 1986.

Gandhi, Mahatma. *Non-Violence in Peace and War.* 2 volumes. Ahmedbad, India: Navajivan Publishing House, 1948.

Gregory, XVI, Pope. *Singulari nos: Encyclical Letter to all the Patriarchs, Prelates, Archbishops, and Bishops.* July 7, 1834.

Halstead, Fred. *Out Now: A Participant's Account of the Movement against the War.* New York: New American Library, 1984.

Hegel, G. F. W. *Philosophy of Mind.* Translated by William Wallace. Oxford: The Clarendon Press, 1894.

Heidegger, Martin. *Sein und Zeit.* Tubingen: Niemeyer, 1967. In English *Being and Time.* Translated by John Macquarrie and Edward Robinson. New York: Harper & Row, 1962.

———. *Basic Works.* Translated by Frank Capuzzi and J. Glenn Gray. Edited by David Krell. New York: Harper & Row, 1977.

———. *Vortrage und Aufsatze.* Pfullingen: Neske, 1954.

Hilton, Walter. *The Ladder of Perfection.* Translated by Leo Sherley-Price. Introduction by Clifton Wolters. New York: Penguin Books, 1988.

Hitti, Philip K. *Islam: A Way of Life.* Washington, D.C.: Regnery Gateway, Inc., 1987.

Hobbes, Thomas. *Leviathan.* Edited by Michael Oakeshott. New York: Macmillan Publishing Company, 1962.

Konrad, George. *The Case Worker.* Translated by Paul Aston. Introduction by Irving Howe. New York: Penguin Books, 1987.

Lamennais. *Correspondence.* Edited by Emil Forgues. 2 vols. Paris: n.p., 1864.

———. *Le livre du peuple.* Paris: Garnier, n.d.

———. *Essay on Indifference in Matters of Religion.* Translated by Lord Stanley of Alderley. London: John Macqueen, 1895.

Luther, Martin. *Martin Luther's Works.* Philadelphia: Fortress Press. 1967.

———. *A Treatise on Christian Liberty.* Translated by W. A. Lambert. Edited by Harold J. Grimm. Philadelphia: Fortress Press, 1957.

Machiavelli, Niccolo. *The Discourses.* Translated and introduction by Leslie J. Walker, S. J. London: Routledge & Kegan Paul, 1975.

Madison, James, Alexander Hamilton and John Jay. *The Federalist Papers.* Edited by Jacob E. Cooke. Middletown, Connecticut: Wesleyan University Press, 1961.

Maritain, Raïssa. *We Have Been Friends Together.* Translated by Julie Kernan. New York: Longmans, Green and Co.: 1942.

———. *Raïssa's Journal.* Presented by Jacques Maritain. Albany, New

York: Magi Books, 1973. Originally published in 1963.

M'Culloch v. Maryland, et al., 17 U.S. (4 Wheat) 316 (1819).

Meinecke, Friedrich. *Machiavellianism: The Doctrine of Raison D' Etat and its Place in Modern History*. Translated by Douglas Scott. New Haven: Yale University Press, 1957.

Mill, John Stuart. *Considerations on Representative Government*. London: Longman, Green, Longman, Roberts, and Green, 1865.

Moses, Jeffrey. *Oneness: Great Principles Shared by all Religions*. New York: Fawcett Columbine, 1989.

Mounier, Emmanual. *Personalism*. Translated by Philip Maret. Notre Dame, Indiana: University of Notre Dame Press, n.d.

Munro v. Socialist Workers Party, 479 U.S. 189 (1986).

Murray, John Courtney, S.J. *We Hold These Truths*. Kansas City, Missouri: Sheed and Ward, 1988.

Mussolini, Benito. *Fascism: Doctrine and Institution*. Rome: "Ardita" Publishers, 1935.

Ockham, William. *A Short Discourse on Tyrannical Government*. Translated by John Kilcullen. Edited by Arthur Stephen McGrade. London: Cambridge University Press, 1992.

Olmstead v. United States, 227 U.S. 438 (1928).

Péguy, Charles. *Basic Verities*. Rendered into English by Ann and Julian Green. New York: Pantheon Books, 1943.

Plato. *The Republic*. 3rd Edition. Translated by Benjamin Jowett. Oxford: Clarendon Press, 1925.

Radhakrishnan, S. *Eastern Religions and Western Thought*. London: Oxford University Press, 1939.

Rawls, John. *A Theory of Justice*. Cambridge: Harvard University Press, 1971.

Rodriguez v. Popular Democratic Party, 457 U.S. 1 (1982).

Rousseau, Jean-Jacques. *Discourse on the Origins and Foundations of Inequality Among Men*. Translated and edited by Victor Gourevitch. New York: Harper & Row, 1986.

——. *Discourse on the Science and Arts*. Translated and edited by Victor Gourevitch. New York: Harper & Row, 1986.

——. *Complete Works*. Edited by Bernard Gagnebin and Marcel Raymone. Paris: Gallimard, 1968.

Schuck, Michael J. *That They Be One: The Social Teaching of the Papal Encylicals, 1740-1989*. Washington, D.C.: Georgetown University Press, 1991.

Simon, Yves R. *Philosophy of Democratic Government*. Chicago: The University of Chicago Press, 1951.

————. *Work, Society and Culture.* Edited by Vukan Kuic. New York. Fordham University Press, 1971.

————. *Practical Knowledge.* Edited by Robert J. Mulvaney. New York: Fordham University Press, 1991.

Solzhenitsyn, Alexander. *One Day in the Life of Ivan Denisovich.* Translated by Ralph Parker. New York: New American Library, 1963.

————. *The First Circle.* Translated by Thomas P. Whitney. New York: Harper & Row, 1968.

Suarez, Francisco. *Defense of the Faith.* Translated by George A. Moore. Chevy Chase, Maryland: Country Dollar Press, 1950.

Sydney, Algernon. *Discourses Concerning Government.* Edited by Thomas G. West. Indianapolis, Indiana: Liberty Classics, 1990.

Tocqueville, Alexis de. *Democracy In America.* 2 vols. Translated by Henry Reeve. Introduction by John Stuart Mill. New York: Schocken Books, 1974.

————. *Selected Letters on Politics and Society.* Edited by Roger Bocschc. Translated by James Toupin and Roger Boesche. Berkeley, California: University of California Press, 1985.

————. *The Reflections of Alexis de Tocqueville.* Edited and Introduction by J. P. Meyer. Translated by Alexander Teixeira DeMattos. Morningside Heights, New York.: Columbia University Press, 1949.

MISCELLANEOUS

Lincoln, Abraham. "Gettysburg Address." Final Draft. November 19, 1863. *Abraham Lincoln's Speeches and Writings.* Birmingham, Alabama: Gryphon Editions, 1991.

Roosevelt, Franklin D. "State of the Union Address" 4 January, 1939. Speech File Box no. 43. Folder Title 1191. Franklin D. Roosevelt Library, Hyde Park, New York.

SECONDARY SOURCES

BOOKS

Adorno, T. *Jargon der Eigenlichkeit.* Frankfurt: Suhrkamp, 1964.

Babbitt, Irving. *Rousseau and Romanticism.* Introduction by Claes Ryn. New Brunswick, New Jersey: Transaction Publishers, 1941.

————. *Democracy and Leadership*. Foreword by Russell Kirk. Indianapolis, Indiana: Liberty Classics, 1979.

Bredvold, Louis J. and Ralph G. Ross, editors. *The Philosophy of Edmund Burke*. Ann Arbor, Michigan: University of Michigan Press, 1967.

Burnham, James. *The Managerial Revolution*. Westport, Connecticut: Greenwood Press, 1972.

Carr, H. Wildon. *The Philosophy of Change: A Study of the Fundamental Principal of the Philosophy of Bergson*. London: Macmillan and Co., 1914.

Colledge, Edmund and Bernard McGinn. *Meister Eckhart*. New York: Paulist Press, 1981.

Deane, Herbert A. *The Political and Social Ideas of St. Augustine*. New York: Columbia University Press, 1963.

Dirscherl, Denis, S.J. *Dostoevsky and the Catholic Church*. Chicago: Loyola University Press, n.d.

De Benedictus, Matthew M. *The Social Thought of Saint Bonaventure*. Westport, Connecticut. Greenwood Press, 1972.

Doering, Bernard. *Jacques Maritain and the French Catholic Intellectuals*. Notre Dame, Indiana: University of Notre Dame Press, 1983.

Dunaway, John W., editor. *Exiles and Fugitives: The Letters of Jacques and Raïssa Maritain, Allen Tate, and Caroline Gordon*. Baton Rouge, Louisiana: Louisiana State University Press, 1992.

Emerson, Thomas I. *The System of Freedom of Expression*. New York: Random House, 1970.

Emerton, Ephraim. *The Defensor Pacis of Marsiglio of Padua: A Critical Study*. Cambridge: Harvard University Press, 1920.

Etzkorn, Dr. Girard. *The Philosophy of Gabriel Marcel*. Edited by Paul Arthur Schlipp and Lewis Edwin Hahn. LaSalle, Illinois: Open Court, 1991.

Farias, Victor. *Heidegger and Nazism*. Edited and Foreword by Joseph Margolis and Tom Rockmore. Philadelphia: Temple University Press, 1989.

Gewirth, Alan. *Marsilius of Padua*. New York: Arno Press, 1979.

Gilbert, Allan H. *Machiavelli's Prince and its Forerunners: The Prince as a Typical Book de Regimine Principum*. Durham, North Carolina: Duke University Press, 1938.

Gilson, Etienne. *The Spirit of Mediaeval Philosophy*. Notre Dame, Indiana: University of Notre Dame Press, 1991. Originally published in 1936.

Griffin, John Howard and Yves R. Simon. Foreword by Anthony O. Simon. *Jacques Maritain: Homage in Words and Pictures*. Albany, New York: Magi Books, 1974.

Griswold, C. L. *Self-Knowledge in Plato's Phaedrus*. New Haven: Yale University Press, 1986.

Hartle, Ann. *The Modern Self in Rousseau's Confessions*. Notre Dame, Indiana: Notre Dame University Press, 1983.

Haval, Václav, et al. *The Power of the Powerless*. Introduction by Steven Lukes. Armonk, New York: Palach Press, 1985.

Horwitt, Sanford D. *Let Them Call Me Rebel: Saul Alinsky, His Life and Legacy*. New York: Alfred A. Knopf, 1989.

Jardin, André. *Tocqueville: A Biography*. Translated by Lydia Davis with Robert Hemenway. New York: Farrar Straus Giroux, 1988.

Iyer, Raghavan. *The Moral and Political Thought of Mahatma Gandhi*. 2nd edition. London: Concord Grove Press, 1983. Originally published in 1973 by Oxford University Press.

Jordan, David P. *The Revolutionary Career of Maximillen Robespierre*. New York: The Free Press, 1985.

Kenyon, Cecila M. *The Antifederalists*. Foreword by Gordon S. Wood. Boston: Northeastern University Press, 1985.

Löwith, Karl. *Mein Leben in Deutschland vor und nach 1933*. Stuttgart: Metzler, 1986.

MacPherson, Myra. *Long Time Passing: Vietnam and the Haunted Generation*. New York: New American Library, 1984.

McCool, Gerald A., editor. *The Universe as Journey. Conversations with W. Norris Clarke, S.J.* New York: Fordham University Press, 1988.

————. *Catholic Theology in the Nineteenth Century: The Quest for a Unitary Method*. New York: Seabury Press, 1977.

Merton, Thomas, editor. *Gandhi on Non-Violence*. New York: New Directions Publishing Corp., 1964.

Mettam, Roger. *Power and Faction in Louis XIV's France*. Oxford: Basil Blackwell, 1988.

Michner, Nora M. *Maritain on the Nature of Man in a Christian Democracy*. Hull, Ontario, Canada: Editions "L' Eclair," 1955.

Milosz, Czeslaw. *The Captive Mind*. Translated by Jane Zielonko. New York: Vintage Books, 1955.

Misner, Paul. *The History of Social Catholicism in Europe*. New York: Crossroad Publishing Co., 1991.

Ozment, Steven. *Protestants: The Birth of a Revolution*. New York: Doubleday, 1992.

Palmer, R. R. *The Age of Democratic Revolution: A Political History of Europe and America, 1760-1800*. 2 vols. Princeton, New Jersey: Princeton University Press, 1959. Reissued, 1989.

Panichas, George A. *The Burden of Vision*. Chicago: Regnery Gateway,

Inc., 1985.

Polk, Timothy. *The Prophetic Persona: Jeremiah and the Language of the Self.* Sheffield, England: JSOT Press, 1984.

Roche, Denis, editor. *Liberty or Death.* Paris: Tchou, 1969.

Roe, W. G. *Lamennais and England: The Reception of Lamennais's Religious Ideas in England in the Nineteenth Century.* Glasgow: Oxford University Press, 1966.

Ropke, Wilhelm. *A Humane Economy: The Social Framework of the Free Market.* Lanham, Maryland: University Press of America, 1986.

Ryn, Claes G. *Democracy and the Ethical Life.* Washington, D. C.: Catholic University of America Press, 1990. Second edition, expanded.

Schoeman, Ferdinand D., editor. *Philosophical Dimensions of Privacy: An Anthology.* London: Oxford University Press, 1984.

Sigmund, Paul E., editor and translator. *St. Thomas Aquinas on Politics and Ethics.* New York: W. W. Norton & Company, 1988.

Skinner, Quentin. *The Foundations of Modern Political Thought.* 2 vols. London: Cambridge University Press, 1978.

Soboul, Albert. *The Sans-Culottes.* Translated by Remy Inglis Hall. Princeton, New Jersey: Princeton University Press, 1980.

Stearns, Peter N. *Priest and Revolutionary: Lammennais and the Dilemma of French Catholicism.* New York: Harper & Row, 1967.

Sterling, Richard. *Ethics in a World of Power: The Political Ideas of Friedrich Meinecke.* Princeton, New Jersey: Princeton University Press, 1958.

Storing, Herbert J., editor. *The Anti-Federalists.* Chicago: University of Chicago Press, 1985.

Suther, Judith. *Raïssa Maritain: Pilgrim, Poet, Exile.* New York: Fordham University Press, 1990.

Thompson, Dennis F. *John Stuart Mill and Representative Government.* Princeton, New Jersey: Princeton University Press, 1976.

Verbeke, Gerard. *The Presence of Stoicism in Medieval Thought.* Washington, D.C.: Catholic University of America Press, 1983.

Vernon, Richard. *Citizenship and Order: Studies in French Political Thought.* Toronto: University of Toronto Press, 1986.

Viereck, Peter. *Shame and Glory of the Intellectuals: Babbitt Jr. vs. The Rediscovery of Values.* Boston: Beacon Press, 1953.

————. *The Unadjusted Man: A New Hero for Americans.* New York: Capricorn Books, 1962.

Walsh, David. *After Ideology: Recovering the Spiritual Foundation of Freedom.* San Francisco: Harper-Collins Publishers, 1990.

Weiss, Paul. *Modes of Being.* Carbondale, Illinois: Southern Illinois

University Press, 1968.

Wolin, Richard, *The Politics of Being: The Political Thought of Martin Heidegger.* New York: Columbia University Press, 1990.

Wolff, Hans Walter. *Anthropology of the Old Testament.* Philadelphia. Fortress Press, 1974.

Zaehner, R. C. *Hinduism.* London: n.p., 1962.

ARTICLES

Adler, Mortimer J. and Walter Farrell. "The Theory of Democracy." *The Thomist* 4, *et seq.* 1941-1944.

Archibald, Katherine. "The Concept of Social Hierarchy in the Writings of St. Thomas Aquinas." *The Historian.* Vol. II. 1949-1950.

Armstrong, A. H. "Form, Individual and Person in Plotinus." *Dionysius* 1. 1977.

Baisnee, Julius A. "Two Catholic Critiques of Personalism." *The Modern Schoolman.* Vol. XXII. No. 2. January, 1945.

Belknap, Robert. "The Structure of Inherent Relationships: The Buffoon, the *Nadryv* (Laceration)." *The Structure of the Brothers Karamazov.* The Hague: Mouton and Co., 1947.

Clark, Mary T. "An Inquiry into Personhood." *The Review of Metaphysics.* Vol. XLVI. No. 1. September, 1992.

Clarke, W. Norris. "Action as the Self-Revelation of Being: A Central Theme in the Thought of St. Thomas." Linus Thro, editor. *History of Philosphy in the Making, In Honor of James Collins.* Lanham, Maryland: University Press of America, 1982.

Creaveny, John. "Person and Individual." *The New Scholasticism.* Vol. XVII. No. 3. July, 1943.

Dallmayr, Fred. "Ontology of Freedom: Heidegger and Political Philosophy." *Polis and Praxis.* Cambridge: MIT Press, 1984.

Dennehy, Raymond. "Maritain's Theory of Subsistence: The Basis of His Existentialism." *The Thomist* 39. 1979.

Dostal, Robert. "Friendship and Politics. Heidegger's Failing." *Political Theory.* Vol. 20. No. 3. August, 1992.

Eschmann, I. Thomas. "In Defense of Jacques Maritain." *The Modern Schoolman.* Vol. XXII. No. 4. May, 1945.

Hughes, H. Stuart. "Marcel, Maritain and the Secular World." *The American Scholar.* Vol. 35. Autumn, 1966.

Judt, Tony. "'We have discovered History': Defeat, Resistance and the

Intellectuals in France." *The Journal of Modern History*. Volume 64. Supp., December, 1992.

McCool, Gerald A. "Maritain's Defense of Democracy." *Thought*. Vol. 54. No. 213. June, 1979.

Nef, John U. "Péguy and the Spirit of France." *The Review of Politics* 5. No. 3. July, 1943.

O' Malley, Frank. "The Evangelism of George Bernanos." *The Review of Politics* 6. No. 4. October, 1944.

Prosser, William L. "Privacy." 48 *California Law Review*. 1960 (1890).

Riley, Patrick. "The General Will before Rousseau." *Political Theory*. Vol. 6. No. 4. November, 1978.

Ryn, Claes. "Historicism and its Critics." *Modern Age*. Summer/Fall, 1987.

———. "Universality and History: The Concrete as Normative." *Humanitas*. Vol. VI. No. 1. Fall, 1992/Winter, 1993.

Shklar, Judith. "Bergson and the Politics of Intuition." *The Review of Politics* 20. No. 4. October, 1958.

Stanlis, Peter J. "Babbitt, Burke and Rousseau." *Irving Babbitt in Our Time*. Editors George A. Panichas and Claes Ryn. Washington, D.C.: Catholic University of America Press, 1986.

Stern, Guenther. "On the Pseudo-Concreteness of Heidegger's Philosophy." *Philosophy and Phenomenlogical Research* 9. 1948.

Strauss, Leo. "A Giving of Accounts." *The College* 22. No. 1 and 3.

INDEX

ABOUT THE AUTHOR

John DiJoseph is a scholar, lawyer, and photographer. He graduated cum laude with a B. A. in history from Catholic University in 1954. He served as a special agent in the Counter Intelligence Corp of the U.S. Army from 1955-1957. He received a M. A. in history from George Mason University in 1989, a M. A. in politics from Catholic University in 1991, and a Ph.D. in politics from Catholic University in 1993.

He is a trial lawyer and a member of the bar of the United States Supreme Court, several federal appellate courts, and the Supreme Court of Virginia. His legal publications include "The One and the Many: The Expropriation of Intellectual Property by the States—Copyright and the Eleventh Amendment," 9 *Loyola Ent. L. J.* 1 (1989).

He was a photojournalist for twenty years during which time he regularly covered the White House and the Congress. He is known for his candid portraits and architectural photography.

Dr. DiJoseph currently is an adjunct professor of history at Marymount University in Arlington, Virginia.